P9-DHF-961

# SHIPWRECKS
## *of Lake Superior*

*Edited by*
**JAMES R. MARSHALL**

Lake Superior PORT CITIES, Inc.     Duluth, MInnesota     1987

EDITOR: James R. Marshall
DESIGNER: Roberta Baker
MANAGING EDITOR: Paul L. Hayden
COLOR SEPARATIONS: Duluth Photo Graphics
PRINTING: Davidson Printing Company, Duluth
TYPESETTING: Lake Superior TYPESETTERS, Duluth, Minnesota

©1987 by Lake Superior Port Cities Inc.
All rights reserved. No part of this publication may be reprinted or transmitted in any form or by any means, electronic or mechanical, including photocopying, recording or any information storage and retrieval system, without permission in writing from the publisher.

Second Printing: 1988
Third Printing: 1990
Fourth Printing: 1992
Fifth Printing: 1995
10  9  8  7  6  5

Shipwrecks of Lake Superior is a publication of Lake Superior Port Cities Inc., also publishers of Lake Superior Magazine.

Library of Congress Cataloging-in-Publication Data
Marshall, James R., editor
   Shipwrecks of Lake Superior
   Bibliography, p. 100.
   Includes index.
   1. Shipwrecks – Superior, Lake. 2. Shipwrecks – Great Lakes. 3. Shipwrecks. 4. Edmund Fitzgerald (ship) 5. America (ship) I. Title.
Library of Congress Card Catalog Number: 87-80682.
ISBN 0-942235-00-2.
Printed in the United States of America

**Lake Superior** MAGAZINE™
P.O. Box 16417
Duluth, Minnesota 55816-0417
800-635-0544

Cover Photo: *A skin diver peers from a bell-mouthed ventilator on the* Emperor *which struck and foundered at the Canoe Rocks near Isle Royale, Michigan, June 4, 1947. Photo by Bruce Bisping*

# *PREFACE*

**C**OME WITH US NOW AS WE EMBARK UPON A
REMARKABLE VENTURE, a diorama of the tragedies
wrought by wind, waves and zero visibility on mighty Lake
Superior.

All vessels are bound by the elements and subject to the sometimes terrible whims of nature. No captain ever embarked upon
this lake thinking his voyage would be different from the many
others he had made. As he viewed the lake from a momentary
vantage point, a captain might have paused to reflect upon the
broad expanse of water to be seen — and ponder the endless miles
of open water between him and the safety of the chosen goal.
Thunder Bay (known as Port Arthur and Fort William to earlier
mariners, and "the Station" to the earliest), Munising, Marquette,
Houghton or Hancock all promised a snug harbor and warm accommodations. La Pointe, the tiny settlement on Madeline Island
in the Apostle Islands just off the present city of Bayfield, Wisconsin, was another earnest destination in the 1600s, when boats
were a frail and tender means of travel.

In the early years, lumber hookers "hauled out" of the mouth
of the Iron River, north of the Wisconsin town of the same name,
and out of Ontonagon, Munising and several other Michigan
ports, to wait at the primitive lock in the St. Marys River along
with ships from all over Lake Superior for access to waiting
markets. Cargoes of copper, iron and fish joined the ever-
increasing stream of wealth generated in the newly settled region.
Dozens of sail-driven vessels called at Superior City (now Superior, Wisconsin), unloading hardware, paint, railroad and construction materials.

On the North Shore, iron ore was first loaded into small ships
in 1884, following the completion of the railroad to Tower,
Minnesota. Tofte, Grand Marais, Hovland and Grand Portage
needed to ship fish and lumber and at the same time receive nets,
furniture, foodstuffs and clothing from the civilized world.

Lake Superior commerce was handled by a sometimes terrified
crew. No means of navigation except a simple compass and a
boxed ship's clock assuaged this fear; each successful voyage stood
as a testimonial to the competence of the captain and his crew.

Grant these early mariners the deep respect they deserve. The
last wreck has not yet been recorded.

*James R. Marshall*
*April 1987*

# CONTENTS

# History of Shipwrecks

# Lake Superior's Commercial Shipwreck History

## *A panorama of the Lake's intriguing hidden treasures*

### by Dr. Julius F. Wolff, Jr.
#### photographs courtesy of Elmer Engman

**VER THE LAST 30 YEARS** public interest in the history of Lake Superior shipping and shipwrecks has increased phenomenally. Historical researchers have cooperated with scuba divers on stories of more than 300 vessels lost since the advent of American shipping in 1835. There have been founderings, strandings, fires and collisions. Approximately two dozen ships have just disappeared, or "gone missing."

Researchers and diving teams have worked out of numerous locations: Sault Ste. Marie, Michigan and Ontario; Whitefish Point; Grand Marais, Michigan; Munising; Marquette; the Portage Ship Canal area and Keweenaw Point; Ashland and Chequamegon Bay; Duluth-Superior; the Minnesota north shore; Isle Royale; Thunder Bay and the Ontario northern and eastern coasts. Wrecks identified during general research have been precisely located and investigated by divers. Priceless artifacts have been retrieved for the numerous shipwreck museums blossoming from one end of the lake to the other.

### THE UNSINKABLE CANOE

The earliest sailing on Lake Superior occurred many centuries ago, perhaps in dugout canoes operated by aboriginal people of a pre-Mississippian culture interested in the copper of Isle Royale or the Keweenaw. In the 1600s and 1700s the fur traders came with their Montreal canoes or Mackinac boats. In the late 1700s some diminutive fur trading schooners appeared, owned by the French or the Northwesters of Montreal.

There is a record of one such schooner being burned by the Americans at the Soo in 1814, while a second, the *Invincible,* was wrecked at Whitefish Point in November 1816 as a result of the Canadian feud between Northwesters and Lord Selkirk's Hudson's Bay Company. When the two factions made peace under the umbrella of the new Hudson's Bay Company, the schooner *Recovery II* was built at Fort William, used sparingly and finally dispatched down the St. Marys River in 1828 for commerce on the lower lakes. For the next seven years

> ***The canoeing record by the Canadians on Lake Superior was almost unbelievable. In a century and a half there is only one known instance of a Montreal canoe being sunk, capsizing off Parisienne Island, Whitefish Bay, in August 1816 with 7-9 lives lost.***

mostly canoes and Mackinac boats would dot the big lake.

The canoeing record by the Canadians on Lake Superior was almost unbelievable. In a century and a half there is only one known instance of a Montreal canoe being sunk, capsizing off Parisienne Island, White-fish Bay, in August 1816 with 7-9 lives lost. The canoe was being manned by Selkirk's mercenary De Meuron soldiers, carrying Northwesters as prisoners and paddled by Iroquois rather than by the usual Huron Indians.

In 1835 the American Fur Company assembled the 78-foot wooden schooner *John Jacob Astor* at Sault Ste. Marie, Michigan, from parts prefabricated on the lower lakes. This tiny vessel, under the captainship of the famous Stannard brothers, served the fur trade on Lake Superior and the developing settlements for nine years. It was lost at Copper Harbor in September 1844 while trying to land supplies at Fort Wilkins during an equinoctial blow. There were no casualties.

With only a smaller American Fur Company schooner, the *Siskiwit,* and a 54-foot fishing schooner, the *Algonquin,* to meet transportation needs for the growing iron and copper mining communities on the lake, shipping companies then proceeded to drag a small fleet of schooners and steamships on rollers across the mile-plus portage at the American Soo. This assemblage of wooden ships was the main line of communication and supply for the pioneer mining villages until 1855, when the first American system of locks opened at the Soo. Thereafter, ships from the lower lakes operated freely on Lake Superior.

*Sunbeam sank on August 26, 1863*

## PIONEERS PAID A HIGH PRICE

These early captains did an outstanding job of navigating the big lake with a paucity of aids to navigation, incomplete charts dating from the surveys of British Navy Lieutenant Henry Wolsey Bayfield (later an admiral) in the 1820s and the utter lack of a weather forecasting system. The goods of the pioneer American civilization were delivered to various ports, but at the cost of a ship or two a year and slightly over 100 lives.

The schooner *Merchant* with 14 persons aboard disappeared in June 1847, possibly near Grand Island; while on October 29, 1856, the 184-foot sidewheeler *Superior* lost her rudder in a gale and was hurled into the Pictured Rocks near Munising, an estimated 50 persons losing their lives. Twelve more went to eternity in August 1862, when the 141-foot schooner *Oriole* was cut in two by the fast steamer *Illinois* in a fog off Grand Island. A catastrophic northern gale on August 26, 1863, capsized the new 150-foot sidewheeler *Sunbeam* east off Ontonagon, and only one man, wheelsman John C. Fregeau, survived out of 27 or more aboard.

Sailing the eastern lake was a lonely experience, illustrated by the disappearance of the large schooner *W. W. Arnold* in the first week of November 1869. The *Arnold* had sailed from Marquette on November 4 with a load of iron ore. She failed to arrive at the Soo. A month later the Indian mail carrier from the Soo reported to the postmaster at Munising that he had seen a wreck at the mouth of the Big Two Hearted River, 25 miles west of Whitefish Point. A four-man search party from Munising went to the spot by coasting and snowshoeing, confirming this to be the ill-fated *Arnold*. She had broken her foremast and was driven aground, tearing out her bottom. Those aboard had no chance in the violent surf.

That the human casualty tolls were not higher resulted from the courage and ingenuity of the pioneer captains. Jack Wilson of the propeller steamboat *Monticello* managed to save all of his people when the vessel was tossed aground near the modern Keweenaw Portage Ship Canal in a violent storm, September 25, 1851. Captain John McKay saved all except four when the steamer *Independence* blew up above the Soo in November 1853. Captain Hiram J. Jones put all ashore when the new steamer *Peninsula* grounded at Eagle River in November 1854. In a stranding at Copper Harbor on November 11, 1857, Captain John Spalding landed his full complement of passengers and crew before the raging snowstorm tore the three-month-old propeller *City of Superior* to pieces, a property loss of $50,000. It was the worst such loss in Lake Superior sailing history to that date.

The largest ship to be lost in the pioneer period was the 237-foot sidewheeler *Arctic* on May 29, 1860, at Huron Islands. Captain F.S. Miller had run the vessel right against the bank of the beach, and all aboard exited over the bow before the raging lake tore the fine ship apart within a two-hour period.

## SHIPMENTS EXPAND WITH COMING OF THE RAILS

A new era on the lake began in 1870. In August the Lake Superior and Mississippi Railroad reached Duluth, and farm products from the upper middle west joined the cargoes. Also, in that year the Riel Rebellion broke out in western Canada, and the Canadians had to send a substantial military force through the wilderness from Prince Arthur's Landing on Thunder Bay. Canadians realized then that a railroad from Thunder Bay to the west was a necessity to hold the Confederation together. The new railhead made Fort William and the renamed Port Arthur major port towns for grain from the prairies, together with some iron ore.

During the decade of the 1870s, the vessel passages at the Soo nearly doubled. Cargoes of iron ore and copper bound for the East were supplemented with grain and some lumber. The Wisconsin Central Railroad reached Ashland in 1877, opening up a vast harvest area of pine. The Marquette Iron Range expanded shipments as new copper mines were developed on the Keweenaw Peninsula. The Portage Ship Canal development was finally completed, augmenting the older ports of Ontonagon, Eagle River, Eagle Harbor and Copper Harbor.

More than two dozen vessels perished in the '70s with more than 80 sailors. However, two monumental gales in 1872, November 12-13 and November 27-28, produced significant changes for Lake Superior navigation. The first storm's northeast pattern shattered the original port of Duluth, built on the lake side of Minnesota Point. The breakwater was breached, spray thrown 100 feet high over Elevator A, and four vessels in supposedly safe anchorage were beached and damaged. Duluthians then realized that any future port development must lie behind the barrier of Minnesota Point, and it is here that the magnificent port of Duluth-Superior materialized.

The second gale, of west-northwest pattern, was far more fatal. The wooden sidewheeler *John A. Dix* and two iron ore-laden tow barges, the *Jupiter* and *Saturn,* were mauled badly by the monstrous seas west of Whitefish Point. The towlines broke. The battered *Dix* managed to round Whitefish Point to safety, but the *Jupiter* was pushed ashore west of Vermilion Point and the *Saturn* approximately three miles west of Whitefish Point. Their entire crews, 15 persons in all, were lost.

The high waves on the night of November 27 caught two grain-carrying schooners in the same area.

The 400-ton *W.O. Brown* was virtually thrown out of the lake at Point Mamainse, Ontario, and smashed to pieces. The 354-ton *Charles C. Griswold* staggered down Whitefish Bay only to founder off Gros Cap, Ontario. Through miraculous good fortune, three of the *Brown's* crew succeeded in getting ashore, surviving in a subzero wilderness and working their way back to civilization over a two-month span. Unfortunately, the entire crew of the

**These early captains did an outstanding job of navigating the big lake with a paucity of aids to navigation, incomplete charts dating from the surveys of British Navy Lieutenant Henry Wolsey Bayfield (later an admiral) in the 1820s and the utter lack of a weather forecasting system.**

*Griswold* was lost. Altogether, 28 men and one woman perished from drowning or exposure. Some might have been spared had there been lifesaving facilities available.

The Board of Lakes Underwriters complained to Secretary of the Treasury William A. Richardson, who responded by instructing a board of Lifesaving Service officers to survey Lake Superior with an eye toward establishing lifesaving stations. The survey was conducted in 1873, the report filed in 1874, and on June 20, 1874, Congress authorized the establishment of four lifesaving stations. These became operational in 1876 at Vermilion Point, Crisp Point, Two Hearted River and Muskallonge Lake (also known as Deer Park). They were manned by the Lifesaving Service/Coast Guard un-

til World War II, saving countless sailors' lives by their presence and action.

Weather problems continued to plague the wooden schooners and steam barges. On October 23, 1873, a mechanical failure sank the new steam barge *Geneva,* downbound with grain from Duluth. Her crew easily transferred to the barge *Genoa* off Caribou Island. Together the vessel and cargo totaled a loss of $125,000, financially the worst in the decade. A collision on August 26, 1875, in upper Whitefish Bay saw the Canadian sidewheeler *Manitoba* ram and sink the Hanna Company's 744-ton propeller *Comet,* with 11 lives lost. The *Comet* was carrying a cargo of Montana silver ore destined for a smelter in Philadelphia, making her a kind of treasure ship. Scuba divers who later located the hulk in deep water discovered that much of the silver had been in buffalo skin bags which had gone through the side of the vessel when she hit bottom. The hides rotted, allowing the silver to mix with the sands of Whitefish Bay.

Rarely has crew discipline broken down aboard an American ship on Lake Superior; yet, such was the case on the 316-ton steam barge *St. Clair* off Fourteen Mile Point northeast of Ontonagon on the night of July 7, 1876. Fire broke out. In launching a lifeboat the captain was knocked overboard; panic ensued, with passengers and crew jumping from the blazing ship into the lifeboat, capsizing it, then fighting each other for positions in the boat when it was righted. Eventually, only three persons remained in the boat, the captain, the chief engineer and a passenger, mayor of Duluth J.B. Sutphin. Later they picked up a wheelsman and a mate riding wreckage. Twenty-six persons perished.

In July 1877, the Canadians lost their first major ship on the lake, the 204-foot sidewheeler *Cumberland,* stranded on Rock of Ages, Isle Royale. Despite an intensive salvage effort the vessel had to be abandoned. Fall storms tore her to pieces. She

Cumberland *sank in July 1877*

had been built at a cost of $101,000 in 1871, worth probably $50,000 when lost. Fortunately, all aboard were saved.

The decade of the '70s ended with an amazing survival exploit by Duluth tugmen and fishermen. In attempting to retrieve the damaged fishing tug *Siskiwit* from Grand Marais, Minnesota, in December 1879, Captain Martyn Wheeler in the 45-foot tug *Amethyst* was caught in a tempestuous snowstorm off Manitou River. The towline broke, and the *Siskiwit* began to sink. Captain Wheeler brought the *Amethyst* alongside the *Siskiwit* in a daring maneuver to transfer her crew. Now there were 11 persons on the *Amethyst*.

A few miles closer to Duluth the *Amethyst* started to sink, and Wheeler ran her ashore at Belmore Bay. All aboard jumped into the surf and reached land, except for one fisherman who was hit by the tug's collapsing smokestack. Though soaked and half frozen, the two crews made huts of spruce boughs, got fires going, dried themselves out and retrieved food from the stranded tug as the seas subsided. The next day the group undertook a two-day, 13½-mile hike through waist-deep snow toward Beaver Bay. The pioneer Wieland family took

the castaways in and warmed, rested and fed them for several days. A Wieland boy with a dog team brought in a member of the party who had frozen his feet and been left in a bough hut. The 10 survivors eventually made their way to Duluth via a small boat. The woodsmanship of these sailors and fishermen, together with the generosity of pioneer inhabitants of Beaver Bay, prevented another "lost with all hands" incident.

## APPEARANCE OF STEEL VESSELS

Big things occurred in Lake Superior country during the 1880s. The timber reserves of northern Minnesota were open to private utilization. A new iron ore range, the Gogebic, was developed in Michigan's western Upper Peninsula, while the first Minnesota iron range, the Vermilion, began shipping through the port of Two Harbors.

Lumber shipping and grain transportation reached new heights. Vessel passages at the Soo tripled, while the registered tonnage of vessels increased four and a half times, indicating larger ships. It was during this time that the first American-built steel bulk vessels appeared. Lake Superior towns and cities jumped in population, with

Duluth achieving a 500 percent increase within a decade. A substantial increase in maritime losses also occurred, with over 50 ships lost and 120 persons dead. Wooden steamships were pushed to the limit, while schooners were converted to tow barges. Breakaway barge accidents were common. And collisions became more frequent.

One costly accident in Duluth harbor on July 19, 1881, saw the 200-foot Canadian passenger steamer *City of Winnipeg* burn at the dock with a loss of four lives. A number of barrels of fine Canadian bond whisky disappeared in the confusion, much to the chagrin of salvagers who had purchased the burned-out hulk.

In mid-November 1883 came the mystery of the decade; the 184-foot wooden passenger ship *Manistee* disappeared en route from Bayfield to Ontonagon. On the sixth day of a giant gale and snowstorm, Captain John McKay, upset with being storm-bound for five days, decided that the worst was past, and he went out. Wreckage from the *Manistee* was picked up along the Michigan coast for several weeks, including a bottle with a note, purportedly from the captain, found at Ashland the next year. Loss of life was estimated at 25 to 35 souls.

Every year brought more losses: strandings, founderings, collisions. A sad incident occurred off St. Ignace Island at the mouth of the Nipigon River, December 13, 1883. The Canadian steam barge *Kincardine* was towing the small American schooner *Mary Ann Hulbert* with a cargo of supplies for a railroad contractor at Michipicoten. The barge carried a crew of five and 15 passengers, railroad construction laborers. The two ships were engulfed by high waves; the schooner gradually sank, taking all 20 persons with her, the worst schooner loss of life in lake history. The *Kincardine* narrowly survived.

The first metallic ship joined the loss list on October 24, 1884. The 231-foot iron steamer *Scotia*, only 11 years old, went off course in a snowstorm and plowed into the tip of Keweenaw Point. She could not be dragged off and quickly broke in two. All of her crew were saved. The lake had proved it could demolish metal ships as well as wooden.

The major financial loss of the entire 19th century came on November 7, 1885, when the 262-foot steel passenger steamship *Algoma* of the Canadian Pacific Railroad crashed ashore on Greenstone Rock off the northeast corner of Isle Royale in a vicious gale and snowstorm. The ship quickly broke up, taking an estimated 48 persons to their death and incurring a property loss of $345,000. Fourteen survivors were aided by island fishermen who flagged down the CPR liner *Athabasca*, which took them to Thunder Bay.

The most unusual rescue on Lake Superior by the U.S. Lifesaving Service came on November 18, 1886. Caught in a roaring snowstorm, the 209-foot steam barge *Robert Wallace*, towing the 217-foot, four-masted barge *David Wallace*, was 100 miles off course when it slammed into Chocolay Beach south of Marquette. Attempted rescue by local citizen volunteers failed. A local ship captain telegraphed the U.S. Lifesavers at Houghton, over 100 miles to the north. At the time the Upper Peninsula was blanketed by heavy snow.

The superintendent of the Marquette, Houghton and Ontonagon Railroad, who had monitored the telegram, offered Lifesaving captain Albert Ocha a special train to take his crew to Marquette. With the railroad line cleared, and daredevil engineer Henry Jackson at the throttle of Engine No. 39, their fastest, the Rescue Special raced out into the tempest at 8:30 p.m., reaching Mar-

*Two monumental gales in 1872, November 12-13 and November 27-28, produced significant changes for Lake Superior navigation. The first storm's northeast pattern shattered the original port of Duluth, built on the lake side of Minnesota Point. The breakwater was breached, spray thrown 100 feet high over Elevator A, and four vessels in supposedly safe anchorage were beached and damaged.*

quette in the unusual time of three hours, 15 minutes. The schedule called for nine and a half hours. After a difficult launch into towering surf, the Lifesavers took all 24 persons from aboard the two stranded vessels. The rescue run had covered well over 100 miles. This record stands today.

The decade of the '80s closed with three breakaway schooner barges in sinkings costing 24 lives. Off Vermilion Point, October 20, 1886, the schooner *Eureka* broke the towline of the steamer *Prentice* and disappeared, taking her crew of six. On November 17, the iron ore-laden 195-foot schooner *Lucerne* broke loose from the steamer *Raleigh* and stranded on Chequamegon Point, her crew of 10 drowning or freezing in the rigging. On September 7, 1887, it was the same story, with the iron ore-carrying schooner *Niagara* breaking the line of the steamer *Australia* and capsizing off Vermilion Point. Scuba divers have located and examined this hulk. The *Niagara* crew launched a lifeboat which capsized, drowning them all.

The latter '80s witnessed a fantastic ship fire at Marquette, with no loss of life, the stranding of a major passenger-freight packet east of Grand Marais, Michigan, with a Lifesaving Service rescue and the stranding and breakup of two vessels at the northern portal of Portage Entry. Again, a Lifesavers' rescue of all on board.

Two collisions marred 1889. On June 19 two sizeable steel steamers collided off Grand Marais, Michigan, the *North Star* sinking the 260-foot *Charles J. Sheffield,* with a loss of $175,000. Fortunately, the captain of the *North Star* held his bow in the gashed *Sheffield* until her whole crew had crossed to safety, this technique to be repeated in following years in steel ship collisions. On July 13, 1889, the 233-foot wooden steamer *James Pickands* sideswiped the 223-foot wooden iron ore carrier *Smith Moore* in a blinding fog off Grand Island. The *Pickands*, whose captain thought damage only superficial, kept going to Marquette, but the badly damaged *Moore* was picked up by the steam barge *M.M. Drake* and was towed to Munising after her crew had been removed. The *Moore* sank just short of Munising harbor and is now a mecca for scuba divers in the Alger Underwater Preserve. [See story, page 83.]

The 1890s witnessed a dramatic increase in shipping: the number of ships doubled, registered tonnage tripled, total freight increased three

Algoma *sank*
November 7, 1885

and a half times. Steel was rapidly replacing wood. A 300-footer was evident in 1890; a 400-footer by 1895; a 500-footer by 1899. Fleets worth millions of dollars began to appear, particularly in the expanding integrated steel industry being fed by millions of tons of iron ore from the mines of Michigan, Wisconsin and Minnesota. An enormous tonnage of lumber was also being hauled, as well as vast quantities of western grain. The population buildup in the Lake Superior area and in states to the west further necessitated a substantial package freight. An additional 60 ships sailed to their doom, although the casualty list was sharply reduced.

The pattern of accidents was similar to that of the 1880s: breakaway schooners going down, a spectacular fire at the Duluth harbor consuming the 29-year-old wooden passenger packet *Winslow* at the dock, collisions of steel and wooden ships, with the latter the worse for wear.

At the end of August 1892 came news that shocked the steel ship construction industry. The 301-foot *Western Reserve* of the Minch interests, Cleveland, less than two years old, suddenly broke in two in a modest storm northwest of Deer Park, Michigan. Twenty-six persons were lost, including the owner and

his family. A superhuman wheelsman, later Captain Harry Stewart, was the sole survivor, able to accurately describe the catastrophe. His testimony enabled marine construction engineers to modify the previously rigid structure of lake ships to permit hull movement. Thereafter, there is not a documented case of a lake ship breaking in two from wave action for 74 years.

The remainder of the '90s brought more schooner strandings after the breaking of lines, some fires, some collisions and several fantastic rescues by the Lifesaving Service. The steamer *C.J. Kershaw*'s crew was rescued by the Lifesaving Service, Marquette unit, on September 29, 1895, in an action witnessed by hundreds of citizens. In mid-October 1898, the steamer *Henry Chisholm* plowed into Rock of Ages Reef, Isle Royale, where she broke up, her wreckage intermingling with that of the *Cumberland* which had sunk 21 years before. Her crew escaped.

The blow of November 21-22, 1898, stranded the steamers *Osceola* and *Harlem* at Isle Royale, and the *Arthur Orr* and *Tampa* along the Minnesota north shore, though all were retrieved.

The decade ended with the 256-foot steel whaleback barge No. 115,

tow of the steamer *Colgate Hoyt*, breaking the towline on December 13, 1899, and floating for five days before being deposited on a reef on Pic Island. Her crew took a makeshift raft to the mainland, then roamed the forest for two days before locating the Canadian Pacific Railroad, where they telegraphed their survival from Middleton, Ontario. The barge was a total loss and was only recently discovered by scuba divers.

## MORE TRAFFIC
## MORE SINKINGS

As the shipping industry entered the 1900s with tonnage tripling over the previous decade, the roster of lost ships skyrocketed, too. More than 80 sailed their last, with a death toll of more than 250, the worst in history. Eight ships took down entire crews and another lost all but one of a crew of 23. Escapes were myriad.

Among major sinkings were the 288-foot steel *Hudson* of the Western Transit Line which capsized off Eagle River, Michigan, on September 16, 1901, taking 24 lives. The 245-foot Canadian steamer *Bannockburn* disappeared November 21, 1902, north of Keweenaw Point, with a crew of 20. And the 291-foot wooden steamer *Iosco* and her 242-foot wooden schooner-barge

*Olive Jeanette* vanished off the Huron Islands on September 2, 1905. Twenty-six died there.

The 262-foot steel grain carrier *Ira H. Owen* was the only steel steamer to founder in the November 1905 blow, taking 19 more to eternity. That November 27-29 hurricane stranded 18 ships and sank one, mostly in the western lake, though some of the stranded vessels were total losses. The death toll by this storm was 31.

One of the decade's more startling accidents was the capsizing of the two-month-old, 420-foot steel steamer *Cyprus* on October 11, 1907, north of Deer Park, Michigan, in a minor storm. Twenty-two men were lost. Second Mate Charles J. Pitz was the only survivor. The crewmen were lifejacketed, but most died of hypothermia in the cold water. Pitz managed to reach shore and was found by a patrolling lifesaver, who carried him to the Deer Park Station where he was revived.

The 1908 shipping season closed with a major shocker, the disappearance after November 30 of the 468-foot steel *D.M. Clemson* west of Whitefish Point. Only five years old, belonging to the Provident Steamship Company of Duluth, with Captain Sam Chamberlin and many of the crew Duluthians, the ship seemed to fade away. Only two bodies were ever recovered, and to this day her demise is a mystery. Her loss of $330,000 was the high for an American ship on Lake Superior up to that time.

The opening of the 1909 shipping season witnessed the disappearance of the 195-foot wooden lumber hooker *Adella Shores*, probably off the Huron Islands, with another 14 gone. To these total losses one could add collisions, fires and strandings which pushed the ugly death toll that year to the worst ever. Indeed, loss of life would have been far worse had it not been for heroic rescues by the U.S. Lifesaving Service as well as by ships' crews themselves.

## INCREASED TONNAGE LOWER CASUALTIES

Severe pressure on the shipping industry during the feverish decade of World War I saw a 75 percent increase in tonnage over the previous decade. The record of 92 million tons logged at the Soo in 1916 was slightly exceeded by the boom year of 1929 and finally broken by the amazing 111 million tons in 1941. Happily, the figure for ships lost was more than halved, though the death

*Rarely has crew discipline broken down aboard an American ship on Lake Superior; yet such was the case on the 316-ton steam barge St. Clair off Fourteen Mile Point northeast of Ontonagon on the night of July 7, 1876.*

toll, increased by nine incidents with loss of all hands, was only slightly below that of July 1900-1909. For the years 1910-1912, only three deaths were noted, these in a collision-sinking of the steamer *John Mitchell* by the steamer *John Henry Mack* in the fog of July 10, 1911, off Vermilion Point.

During the Great Storm of 1913 three lives were lost. The 250-foot steamer *Leafield* of the Algoma Central Steamship line vanished on November 9 west of Isle Royale, taking 18 of the crew with her. It was thought her cargo shifted in the heavy seas. On the same date, Captain James Owen took the 525-foot iron ore-laden *Henry B. Smith* out of Marquette, presuming that the worst of the storm had passed. He was wrong, and sailors guessed that the *Smith* broke in two only a dozen miles out of the harbor. A note found in a bottle the next year, possibly signed by Captain Owen, gave that message. Another 25 were gone.

The next day, November 10, the 377-foot steamer *William Nottingham*, with a grain cargo, struck the Parisienne Island shoal. Three sailors who volunteered to launch a lifeboat and go for help were lost. The death list of the Great Storm might have been worse except for a death-defying rescue by the combined Eagle Harbor and Portage Entry lifesaving crews. The Eagle Harbor men trekked over 30 miles on the windy shore and the Portage crew, 80 miles in the lee of Keweenaw Point to converge on the derelict 451-foot *L.C. Waldo*, impaled on Gull Rock off the tip of Keweenaw. They snatched her 23-person crew from probable death. Every man of both lifesaving crews received the Treasury Department Gold Medal for heroism in this episode. Narrow escapes were numerous in the Great Storm.

The following spring saw a strange disappearance, a mystery to this day, within 17 miles of Duluth. The 239-foot steel *Benjamin Noble* went under with her crew of 20. Later, on November 19, 1914, a complete lumber tow consisting of the 197-foot wooden steamer *C.F. Curtis*, the 191-foot schooner barge *Annie M. Peterson* and the 175-foot schooner barge *Selden E. Marvin* was destroyed by rampaging seas east of Grand Marais, Michigan; 28 men and women went down with their ships.

There were no deaths in 1915, but on May 8, 1916, the 294-foot composite steamer *S.R. Kirby* broke in two in a veritable hurricane off Eagle Harbor; only two men were saved out of a 23-person crew. Her barge, the 352-foot steel *George E. Hartnell*, was picked up by a passing steamer before she hit the reefs.

Oddly enough, the banner years of 1917 and 1918 were free of fatalities for the regular freight ships, but no sooner was the war over than a record number of fatalities were suffered by the French navy when the newly constructed mine sweepers *Inkerman* and *Cerisolles*, just delivered at Fort William, were lost on a

Congdon *sank*
*November 6, 1918*

run to the Soo. Seventy-six French officers and men, together with two Canadian pilots, were swallowed up somewhere north of Keweenaw Point.

As World War I was winding down, the American Tomlinson fleet lost its 532-foot steamer *Chester A. Congdon* on the Canoe Rocks, Isle Royale, November 6, 1918. This was the first $1 million loss on Lake Superior. Fortunately, there were no casualties.

The navigation season of 1919 ended with two heartbreaking disasters. Sometime after November 14, the 281-foot composite steamer *John Owen,* with a grain cargo, was shattered by violent weather near Caribou Island and took 22 sailors with her. On November 22, the lumber hooker *Myron* sank just short of Whitefish Point, as the steel steamers *Adriatic* and *H.P. McIntosh,* along with the lifeboat crew from Vermilion Point, unsuccessfully attempted a rescue. Only Captain Neal of the *Myron,* who had clung to his pilothouse as the ship went down, was picked up alive the next day by the steamer *W.C. Franz.*

On November 14, 17 lives were saved when the 178-foot lumber hooker *H.E. Runnels* stranded and broke up off the Grand Marais, Michigan, pierhead. In a magnifi-

cent display of lifesaving prowess, the Grand Marais station crew, assisted by Captain John Anderson and a sailor from Coast Guard cutter No. 438, in Grand Marais Harbor, together with four Grand Marais civilians, worked a lifeboat up and down a life line against a 60-mile-an-hour snowstorm to the whole *Runnels* crew. The Treasury Department Gold Medal of Honor was conferred on all rescue participants.

## THE TWENTIES
## BRING RELIEF

With peace returning, the decade of the 1920s exhibited a seven percent increase in total tonnage over the war period. Happily, the number of troubled ships decreased by nearly one-third, and lost ships fell by 25 percent. Human fatalities plummeted from a high of 236 to 106, the lowest since the 1890s.

On August 20, 1920, a disastrous collision in Whitefish Bay saw the 429-foot Pittsburgh Steamship Company's steamer *Superior City* being struck and sunk by the 580-foot *Willis L. King.* A financial loss of $650,000 was incurred in this accident, one that is still hard to explain. Tragically, 29 of the crew went down with the ship.

On May 11, 1921, the 194-foot

schooner-barge *Mizte* broke the towline off Vermilion Point and dove for the bottom with her crew of seven. Sometime after April 19, 1922, the 108-foot Canadian lighthouse tender *Lambton* came to a mysterious end southeast of Michipicoten with 19 persons aboard. On the night of November 30, 1922, the 230-foot Canadian steamer *Maplehurst* went to pieces off the Portage Ship Canal, drowning 11 of her people despite the valiant efforts of the Coast Guard motor lifeboat from Portage. Braving tremendous waves, the lifeboat picked up nine of the Canadian sailors willing to jump from their sinking ship. The others refused to leave and went to their death.

In 1923 the 416-foot American steamer *Cetus* rammed and sank the 238-foot Canadian *Huronton* on October 11 off Whitefish Point. The *Cetus* captain kept his bow in the pierced *Huronton* until all had abandoned ship.

On May 18, 1924, the 295-foot American steamer *Orinoco* encountered a terrible snow-laden gale off Montreal Island. Captain Lawrence ordered 17 of his crew to the lifeboats, while he, a wheelsman and the chief engineer tried to beach the stricken ship. They failed. The *Orinoco* headed for the bottom in

15

deep water, taking the three with her. Two other sailors died of exposure in the lifeboats before they reached shelter. The shipwrecked sailors were picked up by the Canadian rafting tug *Gargantua* and brought back to civilization.

On November 5, 1925, the 187-foot wooden pulpwood barge *J.L. Crane* suddenly sank off Crisp Point after the towing post tore out of her steamer, the *Herman H. Hettler*. The six-person *Crane* crew joined the ranks of the dead.

The following year six ships were lost, but all aboard were saved. The season of 1926 closed with two outstanding rescues by the Coast Guard lifeboat from Eagle Harbor. On the snow-choked night of November 30, the 446-foot automobile carrier *City of Bangor* crashed into Keweenaw Point east of Copper Harbor; at the same time the 286-foot steamer *Thomas Maytham* struck a reef on the east side of Keweenaw. The Eagle Harbor Coast Guard first retrieved the *Maytham* crew, then picked up the *City of Bangor* personnel. No lives were lost, but the *City of Bangor* was a total loss, though most of her automobiles were salvaged the next year.

An unusually violent snowstorm with a subzero cold wave marked December 8, 9 and 10, 1927. Wrecks occurred all over the lake. On December 8 at Shot Point near Marquette, the 377-foot American steamer *E.W. Oglebay* was driven into shoals. The Marquette Coast Guard lifeboat bucked ice to take off her whole crew. She eventually was salvaged.

On the same day the 365-foot Canadian steamer *Altadoc*, rudderless, was hurled ashore on the Keweenaw, a half dozen miles east of Copper Harbor. She lost her radio antenna after sending an SOS call, but it was heard by the U.S. Coast Guard, which rushed the Coast Guard cutter *Crawford* from Grand Marais to her assistance. The water was too shallow for the cutter to approach, so the *Crawford* picked up the Eagle Harbor station lifeboat,

which got alongside the *Altadoc* and transferred the survivors to the *Crawford*. The *Altadoc*'s location had been pinpointed only after four of its crew took a lifeboat to shore, then hiked six miles through snow to Copper Harbor. The four, suffering from exposure, had to be rushed to the hospital in Calumet by sled.

During that same storm, west of Isle Royale the Canadian steamer *Martian* was stranded hard at Hare Island. And trying to round Isle

**The major financial loss of the entire 19th century came on November 7, 1885, when the 262-foot steel passenger steamship *Algoma* of the Canadian Pacific Railroad crashed ashore on Greenstone Rock off the northeast corner of Isle Royale in a vicious gale and snowstorm. The ship quickly broke up, taking an estimated 48 persons to their death, and incurring a property loss of $345,000.**

Royale, the 250-foot Canadian package freighter *Kamloops* was somehow disabled and disappeared with her crew of 20. Forty-nine years later her hull was discovered by scuba divers off Twelve O'Clock Point, Isle Royale.

In Whitefish Bay the Canadian freighter *Lambton* smashed into a reef at Parisienne Island. By the time the American Coast Guard was able to reach her, the crew had abandoned ship and reached safety, with

the exception of two men lost trying to make shore.

Spring brought rough weather in 1928. A storm sank the 35-year-old, 199-foot wooden barge *Mingoe* at the Huron Islands on May 21, while a navigational error on June 7 at Isle Royale sunk the veteran 184-foot steel packet *America* [See story page 66]. Passengers and crew escaped in both cases. Loss was modest.

1929 was a different story. The Great Lakes Transit Company lost two ships to a May storm and another in October. On May 15 the 350-foot *J.E. Gorman* was deposited in shoals at Rock River east of Marquette while the 381-foot *Ralph Budd* graced the rocks off Eagle Harbor. The Coast Guard rescued both crews. On October 23 an unusually destructive snowstorm drove the 324-foot *Chicago* out of control for over 100 miles before dropping her on the reefs of western Michipicoten Island. The crew stayed aboard until daylight, then all 32 abandoned ship in lifeboats, taking bedding, tarpaulins and food to the forested shore for an extended campout. Passing vessels notified the U.S. Coast Guard, which responded with the cutters *Seminole* and *No. 119*, successfully evacuating all of the castaways. Damage in all three instances was over $100,000, and in the case of the *Budd*, a refrigerator ship, could have exceeded $500,000.

The final accident of 1929 was tragic. The 251-foot package freighter *Kiowa* was driven far off course by rampaging waves and stranded on a reef just east of Au Sable Lighthouse. The snow was so thick that the lighthouse keepers were unable to see the stricken vessel for some hours. When help did not arrive, Captain Alex Young and four sailors tried to take a ship's lifeboat for help, but this capsized, drowning four of the five. The last individual regained the boat but died of exposure. Later that day lighthouse keepers and some hunters marooned at the lighthouse brought the surviving 19 sailors to shore, where they were picked up by

Emperor *sank*
*June 4, 1947*

the Coast Guard lifeboat from Grand Marais. A loss of $200,000 was incurred.

## RISE OF SAFETY STANDARDS

Since 1930, marine safety has exhibited fantastic improvement on Lake Superior. Altogether, only 17 major ships have been lost from all causes, together with a few fishing craft. The death toll has reached 95, of which 81 were seamen and the rest commercial fishermen or sailboat operators.

Several factors have contributed to this significant accomplishment: stricter qualification of officers, better aids to navigation, more accurate weather information, the improvement of communication, the technological revolution in electronics, better equipped and more costly ships and the consistent monitoring by the coast guards of both the United States and Canada.

Still, accidents can occur. On November 25, 1932, the fishing tug *Lydia* was ground to bits in a terrible storm when she struck the bar while trying to enter the harbor at Grand Marais, Michigan. Five men died. The lives of 122 passengers and crew were endangered when careless navigation caused the stranding of the 259-foot steel passenger

ship *George M. Cox* on Rock of Ages Reef, May 27, 1933. All aboard were saved, thanks to the Rock of Ages Lighthouse crew, the U.S. Coast Guard and a passing vessel that picked up the most severely injured.

On May 1, 1940, the 244-foot steel Canadian grain carrier *Arlington* foundered in the eastern lake, overcome by unexpectedly rugged seas, her captain going down with her when he refused to abandon ship. The 386-foot Canadian freighter *Collingwood* picked up the survivors. A storm 18 miles east of Manitou Island, September 3, 1942, caused a cargo shift on the 250-foot crane ship *Steelvendor*. Listing badly, she took on water in her engine room, cutting engineers off from the controls. Out of control, the ship made big circles for hours in the eastern lake. She was followed by two powerful 600-footers, the *Charles M. Schwab* and *William G. Clyde*. When her engine stopped, the two large ships pulled alongside and quickly took off the remaining 24 crewmen. One oiler was lost overboard during the initial flooding. The *Steelvendor* eventually sank in deep water.

An equinoctial storm on September 22, 1942, caused the tow tug *John Roen* to lose two pulpwood barges, the 254-foot steel *City of St. Joseph* and the 254-foot iron *Transport*.

The Eagle Harbor Coast Guard crew rescued the seven men on the *Transport,* but the *City of St. Joseph* sank and her crew took to the water. The captain's wife drowned, but five others rode logs to shore, then thrashed through brush to a road and walked in the darkness to Eagle Harbor.

On November 28 of that year the 250-foot Canadian canaller *Judge Hart* struck a bar in Ashburton Bay. Other ships dragged her off the rocky perch after removing the crew. But once in deep water, the *Hart* slipped to the bottom.

Blinding fog on June 1, 1943, contributed to a Canadian collision off Passage Island, the 248-foot package freighter *Battleford* sinking the 356-foot bulk carrier *Prindoc*. All lives were saved. In the same year on December 3, a violent gale drove the 321-foot Canadian grain carrier *Sarnian* into the rocks off Point Isabelle. The Eagle Harbor Coast Guard and the U.S. Coast Guard cutter *Plaintree* successfully removed the crew, but the *Sarnian* was consigned to the scrap yard when salvagers arrived the next year. This was the last ship loss on Lake Superior during the World War II period.

Over the last 40 years only four ships have been lost, although

PHOTO BY SCOTT HECKEL

# Researching the Bottom

The *Seward Johnson* is a state-of-the-art research vessel which has been funded by the National Oceanic and Atmospheric Administration for biological and archaeological deepwater research in Lake Superior. Bill Cooper (shown above), Michigan State University biologist, coordinates the work of scientists and investigators who utilize Sea Link II, the manned submersible capable of reaching depths beyond 150 feet, the scuba diving limit. Sea Link II operates on a cable from the *Seward Johnson*.

Though the *Seward Johnson* is used primarily for conducting biological research, Lake Superior shipwreck archaeologists value the vessel's potential for more efficient exploration of some of the lake's elusive deepwater secrets. For example, the Great Lakes Shipwreck Historical Society, Sault Ste. Marie, Michigan, assisted by Pat Labadie, curator of the Canal Park Museum in Duluth, proposed use of the *Seward Johnson* and Sea Link II in Whitefish Bay. The object of their search: the wooden steamer *Comet*, which sank in 300 feet of water after a collision with the Canadian sidewheeler *Manitoba* in 1875. The *Comet* was carrying Montana silver ore destined for Pennsylvania. Though the silver has long since sifted into the sands of Whitefish Bay, exploring the remains of the *Comet* would add more knowledge to archives of shipwreck history because of new information gradually coming to light with the aid of advanced technology.

In 1985 the *Seward Johnson* was enlisted for a short period during the investigation of the *Kamloops* and other Lake Superior shipwrecks. The project was called off because of unfavorable weather conditions. Instead, a remote video vehicle was dispatched from the *Seward Johnson* in search of the *Algoma* bow [*Port Cities Magazine,* Winter 1985-86]. From the *Seward Johnson* deck, scientists could analyze images generated by the sonar and video camera unit suspended beneath the ship.

"But surface monitoring has its limits," says Labadie. "There is a lot more sophistication and flexibility with the manned submersible."

several others had near misses. Trying to come around the northwest end of Isle Royale in poor visibility on the morning of June 4, 1947, the 525-foot steel iron ore carrier *Emperor* of Canada Steamship Lines smashed into the Canoe Rocks and sank rapidly. Twelve Canadian sailors were drowned, though the loss could have been far worse. Purely by chance, the U.S. Coast Guard cutter *Kimball* was only four miles away when the first SOS came. It reached the sinking site in only 25 minutes and picked up 21 Canadian sailors clinging to rocks or sinking lifeboats. The *Emperor* broke in two, a total loss.

Fog on June 23, off Devil's Island, caused a destructive collision between the 480-foot *Crete* and 580-foot *J. Pierpont Morgan Jr.* Two men were killed and three injured on the *Morgan* as the *Crete* struck the *Morgan*'s bow. The *Morgan* limped into the Portage Ship Canal, and the *Crete* managed to reach the shipyard at Superior.

The Duluth Naval Reserve was terribly embarrassed when their training ship, the *PC-782*, was stranded on a training cruise at Siskiwit Bay, Isle Royale, May 30, 1949, with a heavy contingent of reservists and a group of Minnesota Sea Scouts aboard. A flotilla of Coast Guard cutters, Naval Reserve ships and a Corps of Engineers crane barge rushed to the rescue, and the *PC-782* was taken off to return under her own power to the Superior shipyard for major repairs. She was then transferred off Lake Superior.

Mariners' good luck failed on May 11, 1953. A tremendous gale with blinding snow overcame the 427-foot American steel ore carrier *Henry Steinbrenner* off Isle Royale. She foundered at 6:30 a.m., but the captain had remained on the radiotelephone to the last, calling in some of the giants of the lakes, the *Joseph H. Thompson, Wilfred Sykes* and *D.M. Clemson* (namesake of the *D.M. Clemson* which sank in 1908.) These managed to pick up the life raft and two lifeboats launched from the

sinking *Steinbrenner* with 14 survivors; 17 others had gone down with the ship.

On June 21, 1953, the 444-foot Canadian *Burlington* rammed and sank the 416-foot *Scotiadoc* in Thunder Bay. One man drowned.

On September 12, 1953, the storm gods bid for another victim, the 530-foot steel ore carrier *Maryland,* which stranded off Marquette. Apprised of her trouble, the Coast Guard rescue crew, augmented by

## . . . *November 10, 1975, the 729-foot steel ore carrier Edmund Fitzgerald mysteriously disappeared only 17 miles from Whitefish Point and safety.*

Michigan State Police and Marquette County sheriff's deputies, were already on the shore when the *Maryland* struck. They took off 21 crewmen by life line and the last 12 by helicopter. The giant Coast Guard icebreaker *Mackinac* arrived to drag the *Maryland* to deep water before the lake could tear her to pieces.

### FALL OF THE FITZGERALD

Twenty-two years would elapse before another loss. Several daring Coast Guard rescues prevented major ships from going under during that period, particularly in the spring ice pack of Whitefish Bay.

In a gigantic storm with virtual hurricane winds, on November 10, 1975, the 729-foot steel ore carrier *Edmund Fitzgerald* [See story page 48] mysteriously disappeared only 17 miles from Whitefish Point and safety. The full crew of 29 died, and an $8 million ship was no more. An intensive search by the Coast Guard, other carriers, the Ontario Provincial Police and a Navy antisubmarine patrol recovered a good deal of flotsam and pinpointed the place of sinking. The next year a Navy

CURV III vehicle, operating from the Coast Guard cutter *Woodrush*, photographed the *Fitzgerald* on the bottom [See story page 60] broken into three segments, with the stern section inverted. Shipping people, government investigators and shipwreck scholars still argue over the cause of sinking. The media coverage was probably greater for this than for any other wreck in the history of this lake.

On June 5, 1979, tragedy struck aboard the 730-foot Canadian grain carrier *Cartiercliffe Hall*. Ten miles north of Copper Harbor, Michigan, at 3:50 a.m., a flash fire from a sailor's cabin almost instantaneously spread to the whole stern. The crew panicked and abandoned ship without sending an SOS or MAYDAY. Fortunately, the 588-foot steel *Thomas Lamont* of the U.S. Steel fleet happened along at that precise moment, changed course and raced in to pick up the lifeboat of survivors. The Coast Guard launched a major rescue effort which utilized the U.S. Coast Guard cutter *Mesquite* from Duluth, the Canadian cutter *Griffon* from Thunder Bay, the Canadian survey ship *Bayfield,* the U.S. Coast Guard lifeboats from Portage and Marquette and a number of private carriers. Coast Guard planes and helicopters from Traverse City, Michigan, were also called. Coast Guard fire fighters extinguished the flames on the *Cartiercliffe*. Another ship of the Hall Line towed her into Thunder Bay, assisted by the American cutter *Mesquite* and the Canadian cutter *Griffon*. The most seriously burned crewmen were flown by hospital plane to the University of Michigan Burn Center at Ann Arbor, where six out of seven were saved. Altogether, six men died on the ship and another in the hospital, but 19 survived. The ship was rebuilt at a cost of $6 million. The accident displayed magnificent cooperation between the coast guards of the two nations and among the private carriers on the lake.

We hope it will be our last fatal accident on Lake Superior.  □

# Treasures
# and Diving

*The* Winslow *on fire in the Duluth Harbor, October 3, 1891.*

# Hunting for Sunken Treasures

### by C. Patrick Labadie

**photographs courtesy of
Canal Park Marine
Museum, Duluth**

ONE OF THE BEST-KEPT secrets of the Midwest is the incredible store of treasures which lies beneath the clear waters of the inland seas. The Great Lakes stretch nearly 2,000 miles from Duluth to the Atlantic, containing nearly half of the world's fresh water. They are the abode of literally thousands of sunken craft accumulated over a period of more than 300 years.

The lakes formed a vital route for transportation many millennia before the Europeans came, but it was in 1679 that Robert Sieur de La Salle built the first decked ship on the lakes. The great ships of explorers, fighting men and merchants have criss-crossed the blue waters of the lakes ever since, sometimes in enormous numbers.

Large numbers of those ships have been left behind, the victims of storms and ice, collision and fire or of weakness and age. Some 40,000 ships have been built on the lakes since La Salle's primitive *Griffon*, and a significant portion of them still lie in the protective embrace of the cold waters. Historians haven't been able to agree on the exact number of wrecks in the lakes, but estimates range from 3,000 to as many as 10,000 vessels, depending largely on whether or not one includes tugs and smaller classes of commercial ships. The numbers are staggering by any standards.

The sheer number of wrecks and other archaeological resources in the Great Lakes region would lead us to believe that these sites are not individually important, but nothing could be further from the truth. The majority are shoreline wrecks, so there is little left after decades of assault by waves and windrowed ice, and what remains is usually buried in sand or gravel. The number of wrecks which lie in deeper water, beyond the reach of destructive surface action and ice, is probably less than one-fifth of the total number and perhaps as little as one-tenth, at best a few hundred ships. Most of the deep-water wrecks are old, too; relatively few occurred after the turn of the century, and the greatest number date from 1880 or before, making them doubly valuable.

The unique allure of Great Lakes shipwrecks is their state of preservation, which results from the cold, clean water. There are few other places on the face of the earth which provide so favorable an environment for the preservation of submerged materials as do the Great Lakes. Whereas the maritime treasures of most other nations consist of small portions of ancient ships, here several very old craft have been found perfectly preserved in their watery graves, totally intact with their irreplaceable contents — like three-dimensional photographs from some day out of the distant

*The schooner,* Florida *aground in Marquette, Michigan's harbor, November 17, 1886.*

past. Their cultural value is incalculable! They are much more than just museum pieces of yesterday's naval architecture. They are the graves of our fathers and frozen images of our culture's past. They are like American pyramids!

The wrecks of the *Hamilton* and *Scourge,* lost in the War of 1812, are good examples; the schooner *Alvin Clark* of 1847 or the propeller *Indiana* of 1848 also come to mind. These are immensely valuable wrecks, not because of any treasures of silver and gold, but because of their cultural importance. The *Hamilton* and *Scourge* still lie in 300 feet of water in Lake Ontario with swords and cannonballs on their decks and the bones of their crewmen littered about. The *Clark* was salvaged from Lake Michigan in 1969 after 105 years on the bottom and now lies at Menominee, Michigan. The *Indiana* was found in Lake Superior about 10 years ago, and her machinery was raised in 1982 by the Smithsonian Institution. It should be obvious that other such vessels are bound to be found.

Location equipment has been improved, and new diving technology will enable us to penetrate deeper lake waters in the coming decades. If the resources are managed and protected, the Midwest could have the richest treasury of cultural artifacts in the world. The 300-year evolution of Great Lakes ships could be represented by perfectly preserved examples, with the tools and personal effects of each generation of Americans on board.

That is the real treasure of the Great Lakes bottom lands. There is little precious metal and few valuable cargoes from a monetary standpoint, but our roots are there. There are all of the worldly belongings of immigrant families from a variety of nations bound for America's heartland, the weapons of Navy personnel fighting to keep our flag flying over the territory, the tools and implements of schooner crews, the very bones of thousands of our forebears.

The historical and archaeological communities are becoming alarmed at the rate of destruction of Great Lakes shipwrecks by the sport-diving public. Because scuba equipment has become sufficiently safe and inexpensive for mass use, ever larger numbers of divers enjoy the sport nowadays. This has resulted in accelerated destruction of the most accessible wrecks.

Historians and archaeologists are trying to enlist the help of divers to gather data from the wrecks instead of artifacts and thus insure their preservation. On the American side of the lakes the National Park Service has taken a leadership role in teaching divers the basic techniques for wreck surveys and changing diver attitudes about wreck resources. Canadian sport-divers treat their underwater cultural resources with the respect due publicly-owned national treasures. The divers themselves protect the wrecks and monitor their use; they study and survey them, producing fine academic archaeological reports with methodical research. As a result, they will go on enjoying the same wrecks for decades and generations to come.

The same goal can be achieved in U.S. waters, and most of us in the historical institutions of the region feel that it's time to get on with it in earnest. The next generation, too, deserves the rich and wondrous experience of visiting the Great Lakes' unique time-capsules.

☐

*Diver Gerry Buchanan on the* Gunilda's *stern.*

# The Deep Dive

**by James R. Marshall**
**photographed by**
**Joe Schneeweis**

*THE FOLLOWING
ARTICLE DETAILS A
DEEP DIVING
EXPERIENCE IN LAKE
SUPERIOR. DEEP
DIVING IS DANGEROUS
AND VERY POSSIBLY
FATAL. DO NOT
ATTEMPT SUCH A DIVE
UNLESS FULLY
TRAINED BY AND IN
THE COMPANY OF
EXPERTS.*

**Both the truck and the boat trailer strained under the load, and the long periods of silence brought home the full import of the challenge. . .the dangers they would soon face. The shadowy face of fear was easily imagined in the gloom of the darkened truck. The coming encounter with death preyed on each one, but was not discussed.**

DR. E. Joseph Schneeweis is a professional in every respect. An experienced dentist, his demeanor, calm self-assurance and quick smile put you instantly at ease. Standing in his office in Duluth, you have to work at imagining him in full diving gear dispassionately evaluating the wreck he is exploring at 250 feet of depth in Lake Superior. He has been to this depth 16 times in the last few years.

*Robert Horton inspects the* Gunilda's *port side during the deep dive.*

For those not familiar with scuba diving, we should explain that 100 feet is the practical limit for most divers. Sixty feet is more comfortable and the usual limit for those who venture into the depths. Scuba instructors use the term "martini's law" to describe the effect of pressure. In simple terms, the pressure on a diver doubles with each 33 feet of depth. This is known in the world of diving as "atmospheres," and the effect of each atmosphere is the same as a shot of good liquor on an empty stomach.

Put another way, if you were to take underwater a balloon containing a cubic foot of air, at 33 feet it would occupy a volume of one-half of a cubic foot. This change repeats each additional 33 feet of descent.

In reality, we're dealing with the increasing ability of the body to absorb nitrogen. The air we breathe is about 20 percent oxygen and 80 percent nitrogen, most of which is expelled each time that we take a breath and exhale. As depth increases, the blood assimilates more and more nitrogen producing a lightheaded effect known as "nitrogen narcosis" or, in the romantic, "rapture of the deep." Because of this phenomenon, dives in excess of 150 feet are an impossibility for most divers.

The second — and even more dangerous — effect of nitrogen gathering in the blood occurs when a diver begins an ascent from the deep. The balloon illustration reverses, and tiny bubbles of nitrogen begin to expand. Like good Irishmen on a Saturday night, they gather at the "joints," in this case the elbows, shoulders, knees and hips. This is the dreaded "bends," a long-time killer and maimer of those who work underwater. The only safe way to rid the body of nitrogen while ascending is to stop at several depths and wait while the bubbles leave the bloodstream through the lungs. There is no short cut.

Joe Schneeweis learned about the fabled yacht *Gunilda* in 1973, at about the time he graduated from dental school. He had acquired two diving buddies, Gerald Buchanan and Bob Horton. Many an evening was spent discussing the techniques they must develop if a visit to the deep wreck was to become a reality. Up to now, they had visited most of the well-known wrecks, but none of them had ventured much past the "barrier" of 100 feet.

His longtime friend and fellow diver, Gerald Buchanan, when not diving, lives in the world of medical publishing. A lean and confident man from Duluth, Gerry has been diving since the early 1960s. He owns the most complete movie library in existence portraying the fabled yacht *Gunilda*. As the need for equipment grew, it was usually Gerry who found or came up with the money. Before long all acknowledged he was the team leader. To this intensely practical man, reaching the *Gunilda* became an obsession, a dream, a goal.

None of these young men knew

they were about to make history, and, if they had, it would not have mattered. To dive in the cold of Lake Superior to 240 feet and make color movies just had not been done, or even seriously considered. Gerry also had a fine Bauer "Mako" compressor, the finest portable equipment then available. It was his persistence and determination that finally placed this fine group of divers on the deck of the *Gunilda*.

Robert "Bob" Horton completes the trio. Bob is a geologist with the United States Geological Survey and a specialist in interpreting the magnetic signals of our planet. He is skilled in the art of safe diving, willing to try just about anything but always with a clear plan in mind. Horton really believes in the tried and true art of "buddy diving," where each diver is truly responsible for the safety of his partner. "If you glanced at him," Gerry explains, "you found he was already looking at you and what you were doing."

"Bob Horton," Joe adds, "is a man among men in the world of diving!"

There was a time these three men were better known as Lake Superior Deep Diving Specialists. They were not the first to visit the *Gunilda*, but their film documentation of their many dives presents a complete tour of the deepest accessible wreck in Lake Superior.

Word that in 1975 a diver, King Hague, from Thunder Bay had been lost while diving on the *Gunilda* displaced the formerly light banter which was driving them toward the inevitable attempt to reach the fabled wreck. Stories circulated about incredible wealth left aboard the stranded ship by her somewhat eccentric owner. What had begun as a lark became a deadly serious business; a visit to the *Gunilda* became a goal which the three divers felt they must accomplish. Joe, Gerry and Ken Engelbrecht made the first of their dive series on the *Gunilda*, but as time passed, the team of Schneeweis, Buchanan and Horton became the *Gunilda* team.

Planning such a dive, knowing

death was to be the partner, dispelled the exuberance formerly common to the trio. New and better suits were purchased, redundant breathing systems were developed, camera specifications were examined. If such a dive were to become a reality, a camera would be necessary to prove they had actually been there. A Nikonos was purchased, the best then available. The 50mm lens was tried out on shore, and the results were gratifying. This, they thought, would be the recorder

*Many an evening was spent discussing the techniques they must develop if a visit to the deep wreck was to become a reality. Up to now, they had visited most of the well-known wrecks, but none of them had ventured much past the "barrier" of 100 feet.*

of their accomplishments. Unfortunately, the first camera imploded from pressure on an early dive, before they even reached the wreck. This led to the acquisition of an "Ikelite" plastic housing, well tested at such depths.

One of the first things a diver learns in his training is that water is heavy. He learns the term "atmosphere" as applied to the pressure exerted by the water around him. What we don't think about, we humans, is that air is also heavy, and the pressure upon us is that of "one atmosphere."

As we have explained, pressure affects volume. Translated, this would mean that the common one-quarter-inch-thick foam rubber wet

suit, used by many divers at that time, would be just one-eighth of an inch thick at 33 feet. And, even more important to a diver, the volume of air in his lungs at 33 feet is compressed by one-half. Thus, when he ascends he must exhale constantly or his lungs will burst as the air expands.

Imagine the problem facing the manufacturer of a clear plastic housing to enclose a camera for use underwater. The housing will be opened on the surface for the loading of the camera. The air inside the housing will be — obviously — one atmosphere. The assembled housing will then be taken to depth by the diver/photographer. The seals around the various controls for focusing, triggering and winding the film must withstand incredible changes in pressure. Failure of the housing will obviously destroy the enclosed camera, as well as the exposed film.

Diving to the *Gunilda*, the housing did protect the camera, but at that depth the housing distorted in such a way that the controls would not adjust or fire the camera. This led to several aborted dives, and the bending and adjusting of the housing controls until it became a dependable accessory to each dive. The photos accompanying this article were taken with this equipment.

Gerry Buchanan, in the meantime, was developing an underwater lighting system made of heavy pipe enclosing wet-cell Nicad batteries, with 1,000-watt aircraft landing lights enclosed in pressure-proof containers. By the third season, they had lights, both still and movie cameras and a well-organized plan of systematically visiting the entire wreck over a long series of dives. All of this equipment practically filled Gerry's 24-foot boat. It was time to begin diving in earnest.

The plan was to begin a series of conditioning dives, first at 100 feet, then 120, 140 and on down. Only when the divers could communicate, trust and depend on one another would another, deeper threshold be attempted. At the nether world of 150 feet, darkness was a constant, and no reference existed indicating which way was up and which was down. In each succeeding dive, more safety equipment was added: spare tanks at 10 feet and 30 feet, tanks with spare regulators (breathing devices) at 100 feet, pairs of extra complete diving systems at 150 feet. Each partner evaluated the other, and hours of friendly criticism followed each deeper dive. The jokes and joshing of earlier dives were conspicuous by their absence. In street parlance, they had arrived at the point "where the rubber meets the road."

Along with all the gear, Gerry installed his Mako diving compressor in the boat. They could fill their tanks with good air, but the depth contemplated made any diving tank a short term friend. As discussed earlier, a breath at 240 feet, about SEVEN atmospheres, requires seven times the volume of a breath at the surface. Thus a standard 72-cubic-foot tank, containing air compressed to 2,200 pounds per square inch (PSI) provides almost an hour of diving at 33 feet. This same tank will only support breathing at 240 feet for less than four minutes.

Buchanan, Schneeweis and Horton had much more sophisticated diving gear, twin tanks containing over 100 cubic feet of air. After careful hydrostatic testing and evaluation, a method which actually measures the expansion of a steel tank, they increased the compressed breathing mixture pressure beyond the standard limit. Even with this added capacity, because of the time required to descend 240 feet, careful analysis revealed they had less than four minutes per tank on the deck of the *Gunilda*.

In planning the ascent to the surface, experience had shown that decompression, allowing nitrogen to reenter the bloodstream, must begin with a 15-minute stop at 50 feet. This was followed by a longer stop at 30 feet and yet a longer period

at 10 feet. This last decompression station was different in that the ascending diver breathed pure oxygen through long hoses from a tank in the boat. All of the initial calculations were based on the U.S. Navy diving tables — the only available source. These tables assumed a number of constants: a reasonably young diver, well rested, clothed and diving in salt water warmer than 50 degrees.

The *Gunilda* lay in 240 feet of fresh Lake Superior water, with a mean

*Diving to the Gunilda, the housing did protect the camera, but at that depth the housing distorted in such a way that the controls would not adjust or fire the camera. This led to several aborted dives, and the bending and adjusting of the housing controls until it became a dependable accessory to each dive.*

temperature of 38 degrees.

The drive to Rossport, Ontario, in 1980 was not marked by the normal good humor so common to the group. Both the truck and the boat trailer strained under the load, and the long periods of silence brought home the full import of the challenge. Joe dozed, rousing fitfully to ponder anew the dangers they would soon face. The shadowy face of fear was easily imagined in the gloom of the darkened truck. The coming encounter with death preyed on each one, but was not

discussed.

In an earlier dive, Joe had saved Gerry's life when, as Gerry describes it, "my brain turned to mush!" Joe, doubling as the team medic, realized Gerry was no longer in command of his faculties. He took a firm grip on Gerry's hand and led him up from the dark abyss. Without embarrassment, Gerry describes his last remembered moments on that dive.

"We had descended the vertical cliff of McGarvey Shoal, having heard that the *Gunilda* lay at the foot of the cliff. At 90 feet I swam into a solid object, which gave way as I hit it. It was solid and even blacker than the water around me. I immediately thought of the lost diver who had never been found!"

The three divers, exchanging glances of fear and concern, explored the object with their gloved hands. It turned out to be a buoy, formerly a marker for McGarvey Shoal. Ice or a storm had knocked it and its anchor weight off the shoal, and it had come to rest on a shelf 90 feet down the almost vertical face of the underwater cliff. Working along the shelf, they found no less than five such buoys, each still tethered to its weight. One appeared to be very old, crudely shaped from a log and greatly decomposed.

It was at the bottom, some 245 feet, that Gerry's world began to revolve, or "spiral" in divers' jargon. Advanced narcosis had taken control, and he felt the very real presence of King Hague grasping and pulling on him, urging him to join the endless sleep of the depths.

"It was so real," Gerry remembers, "I KNEW he was there. I could feel him pulling on my weight belt. My little world spun around me, faster and faster."

Gerry doesn't remember anything more about that dive, except Joe holding him at the 50-foot decompression stop and his mind clearing.

"He saved my life, and at least one other diver that I know of," says Gerry. "Joe Schneeweis brought me back."

That earlier experience still accompanied them.

They arrived at Rossport, the nearest land settlement, in the early morning hours. As the rising September sun gradually illuminated the dock, it was apparent that Lake Superior was in a docile mood — a rarity in that part of the lake. Checking the transom drain plug, they launched the boat. Anything needing checking was inspected at least a second time. Contrived busyness delayed the moment when lines would be cast off and the lonely ride to McGarvey Shoal would begin. A light fog obliterated the tops of the surrounding islands. Not a ripple stirred the surface.

The "*Gunilda* Gang," as they had become known, had discovered that two strong elements had to be present in order to dive. Once actively discussed, either they now were present or the dive was aborted, by unspoken agreement. The lake must be flat, and the lights must be in good working order. Early experience had clearly illustrated the role of good lighting to dispel "rapture of the deep," and a calm lake surface allowed for an orderly review of the dive plan and an orderly beginning.

The dive plan was everything. It had grown out of the gradual realization that most of the former — and now dead — scuba divers lost in Lake Superior (and elsewhere) died for one simple reason — no dive plan. The second fact common to most deaths was the attempt to do too much on each dive.

On this dive, the plan was the usual simple one. They would descend the line together, each carrying a necessary item. Bob would carry one light system, with movie camera attached. Joe had another light system, with a 35mm still camera. Gerry, with yet another light unit, was the safety man, scheduled to remain at the descending line. This line had been secured to the wreck during the first dive, after they had snagged the wreck with a grappling hook attached to a dragging line. The descending line was currently

fastened to the railing of the flying bridge, and they would do one simple thing: move the line to the bow where it would again be secured.

Joe was to help untie the line, while Bob took movies of his activity on the bridge. Once it was untied, Bob and Joe would swim forward slowly with the line, all 240 feet of it, with Gerry hovering above them. Gerry would watch for a snagging of the line, as well as observe the general condition of the two working divers. The swim would be a

**No sign of recognition crossed between them. Bob's sightless eyes stared vacantly, as his hands added more and more turns to the already secured line on the bit. Joe watched as the figure-eight turns mechanically grew in bulk with each of Bob's motions, and a grab for his hand didn't even slow the tying action.**

traverse of over 100 feet, during which they would descend from 235 to 245 feet. None of the divers had attempted anything so strenuous at this depth. The normal effort expended usually consisted of triggering a camera while swimming with almost no motion so as not to disturb the sediment on the wreck.

The shadowy skull of death harkened with a grin as the plan was rehearsed once more before the divers splashed into the water.

Another lesson in the peril of deep diving was about to be taught to these intruders.

The routine descent began. Each checked the regulators — breathing devices — secured to the descent line at 10 feet, where pure oxygen would be available on their return leg. More bottles and regulators were at 30 feet, and yet more at 50 feet. With encircled thumb and forefinger, each assured the others that the decompression equipment was in place and in good working condition. Time to push the "basement" button on this elevator.

As was the custom, Bob Horton began a rapid descent with a tug on the line and a solid flip of his fins. Checking his watch, Joe followed. Gerry, with a last glance at the shadowy but lighter darkness above him, started down, keeping the turbulence of Joe's fins close to his face. By common agreement, no lights were yet turned on, to conserve the limited battery power. Bob reached the 150-foot knot first, pausing in the almost absolute darkness. He felt, rather than saw, Joe arrive, and both could tell that Gerry was just above them. The game was about to begin.

In earlier dives, all admitted the discomfort (translated: FEAR) of the abysmal darkness at 150 feet. To conserve batteries, all had agreed not to turn on the intense lighting systems until absolutely necessary. The game soon became who got psyched out first and turned on his light! The trade-off was excessive use of air, while outwardly exhibiting lack of fear. On this dive, Gerry turned his light on first, admitting later it was more from a desire to get the whole adventure over with than from fear. The other two lights blinked on, and the dive resumed.

Reaching the 200-foot knot, they realized they were between the tops of two masts, and the outline of the bridge below was just discernible. In less than a minute they were on the bridge, the glare of the lights sharply outlining the wheel, the binnacle which housed the compass just ahead of the wheel and the engine telegraph sharply outlined in the glare of the lights. As planned, Bob began to untie the descending line from the bridge railing.

Joe photographed the procedure, as planned, and when the line was free, they began to make their way forward, toward the bow. Joe's reaction was immediate: the line was already fouled somewhere. It just would not move. He kicked harder, mimicking Bob's effort. Slowly the line began to move. His mind was already confused. He paused, instinct telling him to think the problem through. Suddenly the spinning began, slowly at first, gradually increasing. Fighting the urge to just close his eyes, he forced himself to review what was happening to him. Narcosis. It had to be.

Though almost totally confused, he forced himself to focus on a solid object, the deck just below him. The spinning sensation gradually disappeared to reveal an even more disconcerting fact: the line, and Bob, were no longer in view.

Gerry, the observer, watched the separation of his two friends. His mind was somewhat fogged by the pressure, but the danger was very apparent. The plan had called for Bob and Joe to stay together, and now they were separated. Whom, his confused mind asked, should he assist?

The question was resolved by an upward glance from Joe. No signal was necessary, both realized their diving buddy Bob Horton had forged ahead, unaware that Joe had stopped to deal with his "rapture of the deep." They grasped each other's hand, and began to swim toward the bow of the *Gunilda.* Soon Horton's light was visible, and they found him tying the line to the forward bit. Swimming down to him, they exchanged glances after patting him on the shoulder. He didn't react, or look at them. He seemed preoccupied by the task he was engaged in. A sharp rap on his tanks went unnoticed. Exasperated, Joe bent over, holding his light and his face next to Bob's mask.

*His mind was already confused. He paused, instinct telling him to think the problem through. Suddenly the spinning began, slowly at first, gradually increasing. Fighting the urge to just close his eyes, he forced himself to review what was happening to him.*

No sign of recognition crossed between them. Bob's sightless eyes stared vacantly, as his hands added more and more turns to the already secured line on the bit. Joe watched as the figure-eight turns mechanically grew in bulk with each of Bob's motions, and a grab for his hand didn't even slow the tying action.

Joe glanced at his watch, studying the dial. They had already been here eight minutes — both air and safety were running out. Striking Bob with all the force he could muster, he realized his friend was there in body only; his thought process had long since succumbed to the siren of death. The mind of Bob Horton was no longer part of his body. He was moments from the next phase of nitrogen narcosis, which would tell him to stop breathing. Joe was struck with the peaceful vacant stare. In his confused state, it was appealing.

A glance at Gerry told him that he too realized what was happening. They both grabbed Bob's tanks and, pulling on the line, tried to wrest him free of the line he was aimlessly tying.

Bob Horton simply would not let go!

Joe knelt down near Bob's hands. Grabbing both, he pried them from the bit and the line. Gerry was pulling, and suddenly they broke free of the deck and started up. It seemed like an eternity, but finally the 50-foot decompression station was reached. Gerry's tanks were almost empty, and he eagerly sucked air from the first regulator he could grab. Joe, still with air, studied Bob through his mask. Bob was breathing, apparently without effort. No sign of recognition passed between them. They settled down to wait the prescribed five minutes.

Ascending to the 30-foot level, Horton still showed no sign of being part of the real world. After a few minutes, however, he seemed to be trying to focus on his surroundings, and soon he accepted the proffered decompression regulator, gulping at the volume of air now available. The ascent to the 10-foot station was without incident. Pure oxygen was now at hand, and 20 minutes at the last decompression stop passed uneventfully. Horton was almost himself as they climbed aboard the boat. No one spoke; there was nothing to say. Glancing around, Joe realized a solid fog enclosed them.

Unseen, but clearly felt, the visage of death submerged, returning to the depths to await another unsuspecting intruder.                    □

*Elmer Engman*

# Diving Is Not the Only Danger

## Experiences of a diver's diver

**E**LMER ENGMAN'S FIRST book was *An Underwater Guide To The Western Half Of Lake Superior,* published in 1974. It was the first accurate guide to diving in Lake Superior. Elmer Engman learned to dive in 1968 and found it an increasingly enjoyable sport. What is more important, he wanted to share the sport with others.

A partnership that launched the first dive boat in use at Isle Royale whetted his interest. He founded the first newspaper about Lake Superior diving, the *Nordic Diver,* in 1972, attracting an audience who wanted factual information about shipwrecks of the lake. But the market never grew to make the *Nordic Diver* a financial success.

As word of his knowledge spread, Elmer was asked to share his experiences with an ever-growing audience. Books were a logical outgrowth, and to date he has published three. The original guide was followed by *In the Belly of a Whale* and *Shipwreck Guide to the Western Half of Lake Superior.*

While others pondered the location of obscure wrecks, Elmer tramped many a mile in the rugged wilderness of the North Shore, Michigan's Keweenaw Peninsula and the Ontonagon area to verify locations. He is a good listener, gaining the confidence of local residents who assist him in locating long lost wreckage.

While most divers recall unsettling events underwater, Elmer feels the most terrifying moments he experienced took place on the surface. "Underwater, you have some control," he recounts, "but on the surface, you have no control if the weather is against you." In the *Sand Bay,* his 38-foot Bayfield-built converted fishing boat, he left the Duluth entry bound for a dive on the *Thomas Wilson* [see story page 75]. This whaleback, lying off the

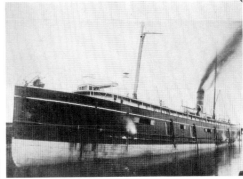

Top, right: *The historical* Algoma. **Bottom right:** *Wreckage of the* Algoma, *which sank on November 7, 1885, lies near the old Rock Harbor Lighthouse on Isle Royale.* **Left:** *The* Madiera, *a steel ship, is still susceptible to the lake's power. Since it sank near Split Rock Lighthouse in 1905, a good part of the ship's hull has been destroyed by wave action.* Photos from Elmer Engman Collection

Duluth entry, is the subject of his book *In the Belly of a Whale.*

Encountering the waves of a dying northeast storm, the *Sand Bay* found herself in the closely spaced steep waves peculiar to that point where the piers end in the open lake. Having risen on the first wave, she dropped into the following trough. The problem was, there was no time to rise on the second wave. Bravely the little boat plunged into the second wave, forcing open a bow window that had not been properly secured. Green water poured in, causing Elmer to reflect that he might soon be able to dive on HIS OWN BOAT!

His diving buddy, Randy Bradford, fought his way to the window, drenched by torrents of ice-cold water in the process. There was nothing to do but press on, since trying to turn around would have put the boat in even more danger.

Bradford finally closed the win-dow, but not before everything in the cabin was soaked. Once out in the open lake it was possible to come about safely, and they began their return trip. Elmer admits that the experience sorely tested any religious conclusions he may have made.

Danger underwater is a fact of life. Elmer stresses the "buddy system" in the classes he now teaches and insists his students learn the real facts about diving, not just the answers to a quiz. His skill is so well recognized that he teaches scuba diving at the University of Minnesota, Duluth. His newsletter, "Inner Space Diving Letter," is widely read. He organizes exotic diving trips to the Caribbean, holds regular showings of excellent diving films and spends countless hours researching the still-missing wrecks of Lake Superior.  □

# Individual
# Wrecks

**Above:** *Diver ascending the mast of the ship* Emperor, *which is located near Canoe Rocks, Isle Royale National Park, Lake Superior.* Photo by Jerry Eliason **Opposite page, top:** *Three-masted boat on Lake Superior, circa 1900.* **Bottom:** *Divers in deep decompression.* Photo by Gerry Buchanan

# Ships That No Longer Sail

## *Sketches of Lake Superior's most popular shipwrecks*

by James R. Marshall
photography by Jerry Eliason,
Gerry Buchanan and
Joe Schneeweis

**W**ITH EACH DIVE THE question again emerges from the closet of the mind: "Who will win this time, the observer or the environment?" Though a diving buddy hovers near you, the tightness of the gut persists and it is with trepidation that you descend deeper in the lake.

Another dive into the green-tinted water of Lake Superior, another challenge to the god of cold and the goddess of pressure. Pressure is indeed a goddess, since her presence is marked with a distortion of normal human senses, known to divers as "rapture of the deep" and to medicine as "nitrogen narcosis." Keep these hazards in mind, but fear not for yourselves as we take you on a tour of some of Lake Superior's more famous wrecks.

As you stand at the base of Split Rock Lighthouse, now a state park on Minnesota's north shore, the view to the northeast is of a rugged point. Known as Gold Rock, this formidable cliff is the gravestone of the *Madeira*, whose torn remains lie just offshore.

As was common in the early years of this century, unpowered barges were towed behind steamships. It was felt this system moved more iron ore for less cost, which usually proved to be the case. The *Madeira* was just such a barge, 436 feet long and built of steel. She lived at the end of a towline behind the *William Edenborn,* an almost new 478-foot Pittsburgh Steamship ore freighter. In the midst of the infamous storm of November 1905, this towline parted around 3 a.m. on the 28th. The helpless *Madeira,* having no engine, drifted in the snow-filled darkness toward shore. With a resounding crash the vessel struck Gold Rock and began breaking up.

The crew found they were alongside a cliff, which towered above them into the darkness. Seaman Fred Benson, about to become a hero, leaped from the deck of the *Madeira* to the cliff, gradually making his way to the top. From this position of safety he tossed the end of a line he had carried, which provided escape for three of the crew. Working his way to a position above the stern, he rigged another line, which provided an escape route for five more. One man, James Morrow, was washed overboard and perished.

The *Madeira* broke into two main sections, both sinking just offshore. Her battered remains lie in from five to 145 feet of water. The wreckage was acquired in the early 1960s by a Duluth salvage firm, which began cutting her up for scrap. Little came of this effort, but the barge they used is beached at Little Two Harbors just southwest of Split Rock Lighthouse.

Having power was of no help to the *William Edenborn.* She went ashore about the same time as the *Madeira* at

**Top:** *Unpowered barge* Madeira. **Middle:** *Deck of the* Samuel P. Ely *in 15 feet of water.* Photo by Jerry Eliason **Bottom:** Samuel P. Ely, *circa 1890.*

the mouth of the Split Rock River. The bow was literally in the woods, where the crew survived with the loss of only one man. The *Edenborn* broke up but was later salvaged.

Dozens of two- and three-masted schooners entered Lake Superior commerce between 1865 and 1890. Built of wood, these small wind-powered vessels were losing out to larger steam-powered wood and steel vessels. By 1890, most were reduced to the role of being a towed barge, while others were just abandoned. One such schooner/barge, the 200-foot three-masted *Samuel P. Ely,* was dutifully following the *Hesper* from Duluth to Two Harbors. The *Hesper* had taken on a load of grain in Duluth and was to tow the *Ely* to Two Harbors for a cargo of iron ore. The extremely violent storm of October 30, 1896, caught them en route, a challenge the *Hesper* barely surmounted.

As the *Hesper* entered Two Harbors, her line to the *Ely* either parted or was simply cast off too soon. Before the D&IR tug *Ella G. Stone* could get a line on her, the *Samuel P. Ely* crashed against a contractor's anchored scow and then the west breakwater. She began to break up almost immediately. Nothing could be done. Lifesaving equipment and a rescue crew were ordered from Duluth, but storm washouts blocked the railroad connecting the two cities. As the *Ely* settled to the bottom, her crew and two from the scow took what shelter they could in the rigging and top masts. They were finally removed to safety by the *Ella G. Stone,* Captain Joe Cox in command, and a small sailboat owned and crewed by a local fisherman.

No attempt was made to salvage the *Ely,* and she was gradually forgotten until she became part of a new west breakwater, which was actually built over a portion of her hull.

Some very enterprising scuba divers located her in 30 feet of water in 1962. She was found to be in excellent condition, and word soon

*Pilot house of the* Madeira *at 90 feet.* Photo by Jerry Eliason

went out, which attracted divers from near and far. The finders, who had the necessary boat to get to the *Ely,*

### The helpless Madeira... drifted in the snow-filled darkness toward shore.

charged them a nominal sum for the short trip. "Only $2.50, each way, mate. Most of 'em swim back...but if we have to make a special trip to you when you're not quite able to finish the swim — that's an extra $3.00!"

Every visiting diver was amazed to

find dishware and silverware, in seemingly endless quantities. More and more divers came, each returning home with a plate or two and a battered knife or fork. After a year and literally hundreds of divers, questions began to be raised in the Twin Cities as to just how large the crew of the *Ely* must have been, since the supply of dishware seemed endless. Only when a plate was found still bearing a sticker "Duluth Goodwill Store — 10 cents" was the salting of the wreck discovered. Traffic died almost immediately, forcing the entrepreneurs to find another method of mining the wallets of eager skindivers.

The *Samuel P. Ely* remains one of the most visited wrecks on the North Shore, being accessible in any weather on the inside of the west breakwater.

Lying far off the eastern end of the north shore of Isle Royale, the Canoe Rocks project slightly above the surface of the lake. While southwest of the normal steamer track between Isle Royale and the entrance to Thunder Bay, during conditions of limited visibility they present a real danger. The first major victim of Canoe Rocks was the fine steel vessel *Chester A. Congdon*, downbound from Fort William (now Thunder Bay) with grain. The lake was in a bad mood November 6, 1918, and visibility was very poor. Stranding on the rocks, the *Congdon* broke up, never to be salvaged. Though her crew was saved, she became the first million-dollar ship and cargo loss.

The lighthouse at Blake Point, on the northeast end of Isle Royale, was modified to show a red light to any vessel approaching from a direction that could put it on Canoe Rocks. This seemed to work until June 4, 1947, when the Canada Steamship Lines' 525-foot *Emperor* struck the rocks.

The *Emperor* had left Port Arthur following the well-worn course all downbound steamers must follow, but obviously she missed a turn. The weather was bad, vision almost non-existent. The impact was violent, causing the ship to break at No. 4 hatch. She sank swiftly, taking Captain Eldon Walkinshaw and 11 of the crew with her.

Twenty-two others were rescued almost by pure luck. An American vessel, the *Kimball* of the U.S. Coast Guard, was nearby and quickly responded to the distress call. The *Emperor* was not salvaged, and her stern, now in almost 180 feet of water, hangs over a deep chasm in the lake bottom.

An unusual story is often told about this wreck. Allegedly the safe was recovered in the mid-1960s by a diver from southern Wisconsin. Rumors persist about some degree of wealth being found in the safe, but this has never been confirmed by Canada Steamship. Little reason exists for any great amount of cash to have been on board. A small safe was visible adjacent to the dock at Belle Isle, the nearest campground to Canoe Rocks. Lying in shallow water, its door open, it was noted by many in the early 1970s.

**Top:** *525-foot Emperor, circa 1945.*
**Middle:** *Crew cabin on the* Emperor *at 140 feet.* Photo by Jerry Eliason
**Bottom:** *Stern of the* Emperor *at 140 feet.* Photo by Jerry Eliason

*The* Gunilda, *circa 1910.*

At the top of Lake Superior lies the tiny hamlet of Rossport, Ontario, clinging to a precarious existence as a former railroad town. Home of some fine fishing and spectacular scenery, the little town was the scene of great activity commencing on August 11, 1911. That's when the magnificent yacht *Gunilda* struck McGarvey Shoal, climbing partly out of the water. The 190-foot vessel, built in Leith, Scotland, was owned by William L. Harkness, one of the original investors in Standard Oil. Their 1910 cruise had previously taken them to Lake Superior, but they had returned this year without the knowledgeable pilot who had accompanied them on their first trip.

It seems they had stopped for coal at Jackfish Point, east of Rossport, and had attempted to engage the services of a local fisherman to guide them to Rossport. His fee of $15 plus return rail fare was deemed outrageous by Harkness, and the *Gunilda* proceeded to her appointment with the shoal without a competent guide.

After the grounding, Mr. Harkness and a crew member went into Rossport

in the yacht tender, a 45-foot gas boat. The insurance company was notified, and they quickly engaged the Thunder Bay Towing and Wrecking Company to proceed with salvage of the *Gunilda*. James Whalen, owner of the firm, set out with the large steam tug *James*

**Albert Falco, a seasoned** Calypso **crew member, after examining the** Gunilda **with a small submarine, pronounced it "the finest sunken ship I have ever seen."**

*Whalen* and the barge *Empire*. "Just along for the ride" was Captain Con Flynn, who happened to be in Port Arthur when the call for help came in. He related the following version of the salvage attempt some years later.

Arriving at the wreck site, Whalen completed his inspection of the *Gunil-*

*da*. In his opinion the wreck would probably come off the shoal with enough pulling, but would go through a period of great instability in the process. He recommended that a second barge be brought to the site, so that one barge could be secured on each side of the rear of the ship. With cables slung beneath the propeller shaft, they would carry the *Gunilda* through the relaunching and provide support if any further problems were encountered.

Flynn claimed Harkness was livid over the proposal. "You just want to charge me for another trip to Port Arthur," he said. "I won't hear of such a thing!" After further discussion he concluded with a final point: "She went on by herself . . . and she'll come off by herself!"

Jim Whalen carefully wrote out a complete release of any liability, to protect himself and his company. After Harkness signed the paper and his signature was witnessed by several people, Whalen ordered that the *Gunilda* be closed up in every manner possible and that all passengers and crew be evacuated. Again Harkness proved difficult, but finally everyone left the yacht.

The towing hawser, a 13-inch Manila line, was secured to the stern tow bit of the yacht. With much black smoke and maneuvering, the *Whalen* was finally in position. But due to the way the shoal was lying, the towing strain was not directly aft, but at a shallow angle. Captain Whalen stationed two deck hands with fire axes at the point where the towline crossed the tug's stern. "If I blow a long one," he told them, "chop the towline off."

Full power was applied, and the *Gunilda* finally began to move. Almost immediately she assumed a list to her starboard (right) side and her stern settled into the water. Whalen had been right; too much of the yacht was out of the water, and the stern lacked sufficient buoyancy to support itself. The list to starboard increased, and the crowd in the many boats that had gathered to watch the event began to shout. As her main deck slid beneath the surface, water poured into several open gangways and portholes. The *Gunilda* was indeed leaving the shoal, but her destination was the bottom.

Whalen sized up the situation quick- ly, noting that while the *Gunilda* was still moving off the shoal, fully a third of her was under water, and the starboard list was increasing. To stay tied to the huge yacht was suicide for his tug, and he grasped the whistle cord. The two deck hands, standing transfixed by the sight of the sinking yacht, responded to the whistle blast. Like beings possessed they hacked away at the towline as Whalen released the towing pressure.

Amid the gaping stares of Harkness, the spectators and the crew on the tug and scow, the *Gunilda* continued to slide deeper into the water, now lying almost completely on her side. With bursts of air and massive bubbles, she settled lower, finally free of the shoal. Though she continued to sink, it was apparent she was righting herself, her design and the weight of her engines restoring her natural stability. Thus, on August 31, 1911, the *Gunilda* slipped from sight to the watery tomb that still holds her, 240 feet below the pinnacle of McGarvey Shoal.

The last comment from Mr. Harkness was noted by Oscar Anderson, then proprietor of the Rossport Inn. Turning to his captain, Harkness said, "Don't worry, they are still build- ing yachts!" With their guests and crew, Mr. and Mrs. Harkness boarded an eastbound train. Out in lonely Schreiber Channel, the last few bubbles surfaced.

Years passed and numerous salvage efforts were discussed, but discussion was about the extent of the activity. In the early 1960s Ed Flatt, then a retired railroader living in Port Arthur, embarked on the first serious salvage attempt of the *Gunilda*. He bought a bascule bridge engine in Selkirk, north of Winnipeg. His plan was to mount the engine on Copper Island, near the *Gunilda*, and pull her into shallower water. Salvage would be simple, he reasoned, if the ship were just in shallower water. Though he spent a great deal of money, and had assembled a fine crew, the *Gunilda* never moved.

Other attempts are still under consideration, and the wreck has claimed or maimed some good divers because of its great depth. Few scuba divers go deeper than 150 feet; the recommended safe limit is 130 feet, which is not even to the top of the *Gunilda*'s masts. [See story "The Deep Dive," page 24]

*Deck of the* Gunilda *at approximately 240 feet.* Photo by Gerry Buchanan

## "...On August 31, 1911, the Gunilda *slipped from sight to the watery tomb that still holds her, 240 feet below the pinnacle of McGarvey Shoal."*

**Above:** *Stern of the* Gunilda. Photo by Joe Schneeweis
**Below:** *Spotlight on the deck of the* Gunilda.
Photo by Gerry Buchanan

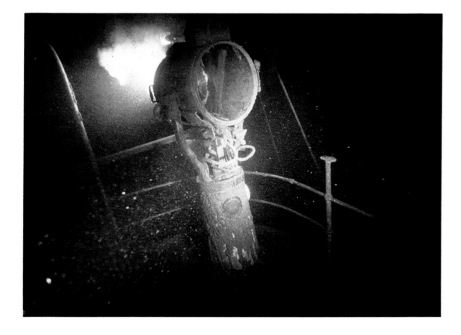

One visitor to the wreck was Jacques Cousteau's *Calypso,* which visited Lake Superior in 1980. Albert Falco, a seasoned *Calypso* crew member, after examining the *Gunilda* with a small submarine, pronounced it "the finest sunken ship I have ever seen."

One cannot leave this wreck without mentioning the fabulous treasure alleged to be aboard. The rumored $200,000 of the 1960s has grown to more than $500,000, undoubtedly placed there by William Harkness' ghost. With plenty of time to remove anything of value, it would pay any would-be salvor to check and see just what the insurance company actually paid for. We can assume some sterling silverware is aboard and perhaps some fine china. It doesn't seem logical, however, to credit this thrifty man with the oversight of leaving valuables aboard a vessel he thought might sink! But if intrigue is your game, remember that few people of substance trusted banks in those days, and who really knows what valuables might be in the hidden safes of the *Gunilda?*

41

## Powered Ships

Earlier we considered the plight of an unpowered vessel helplessly trying to cope with an angry lake. At some point those aboard must resign themselves to their impending fate. Reflect now on the emotional gamut facing those aboard a powered ship when rocks remove the propeller without stranding or beaching the vessel in the process.

The Algoma Central's *Theano,* a 255-foot freighter, found herself in just this position on November 17, 1906, when she struck jagged rocks in a blinding snowstorm. After the power was lost she lurched on, finally grounding herself against Marvin Island near the entrance to Port Arthur, where she began breaking up immediately. Great effort was expended trying to keep her afloat, but after several hours the crew, under Captain G. Pearson, elected to abandon her. They left the wreck in two boats, one of which was picked up almost immediately, though almost by chance. The steamer *Iroquois* found them, but the other boat was forced to row all the way to Port Arthur, exposing those aboard to hours of numbing cold.

No trace was ever found of the *Theano,* which slipped from the rugged shore perch to keep her appointment with the shadowy depths of Lake Superior.

The general location of the wreck is the eastern side of Thunder Cape, known to many as The Sleeping Giant. To these fretful waters came a small group of divers in May 1981. Beginning at the officially reported location of Trowbridge Island rocks, they searched for traces of the *Theano,* but found nothing. The search continued until, to their surprise, they came upon a 14-foot diameter propeller. The main propeller was located in 55 feet of water, but shortly thereafter they found the one missing blade at 95 feet. Although exploration continued to

*continued on page 44*

**Above:** *Underwater reef near the* Theano, *representing underwater terrain near Isle Royale and the Canadian north shore.*
**Right:** *Propeller of the* Theano *at 55 feet.*
Photos by Jerry Eliason

*Land view of Trowbridge Island and surroundings.* Photo by Jerry Eliason

**No trace was ever found of the Theano, which slipped from the rugged shore perch to keep her appointment with the shadowy depths of Lake Superior.**

**Later depth finder chart recordings . . . revealed a large object at 320 feet.**

*Propeller bushing (at 50 feet) of the* Theano. Photo by Jerry Eliason

## SHIPS THAT NO LONGER SAIL

depths exceeding 160 feet, no trace was found of the main wreck.

Later depth-finder chart recordings, a sort of moving picture of the bottom of the lake, revealed a large object at 320 feet. More than likely, it is the *Theano,* far too deep for exploration.

If it is, the *Theano* is in splendid company, including the steamer *Leafield,* Lake Superior's own "Flying Dutchman."

As commerce developed on Lake Superior, many ships sought the port of Munising, Michigan, far to the southeast of the *Theano's* demise. The sheltered harbor afforded by Grand Island was a natural, and this idyllic shelter was mentioned in even the earliest diaries of explorers.

While the location was different, the conditions causing travail upon the lake were the same. High winds, waves and poor visibility all contributed, and Munising received almost more than her fair share of shipwrecks; in excess of 50 vessels came to grief in the immediate vicinity. This has attracted

**Top:** *Deck of the* Granada *in Murray's Bay of Grand Island.* **Middle:** *Deck of the* Granada. **Bottom:** *Stern of* Granada. Photos by Jerry Eliason

44

*Deck of the* Smith Moore.
Photos by Jerry Eliason

Smith Moore, *circa 1885.*

*Propeller of* Smith Moore *at 105 feet.*

Smith Moore *prop-shaft connecting rods.* **Bottom:** W.C. Moreland *at 40 feet.*

both the historian and the diver. Sadly, looting went on constantly until the Alger Underwater Preserve was established in 1980. [See separate story, page 83.] The three views of the *Granada,* which lies in shallow water, show the result not of ice but of underwater vandalism. Frederick Stonehouse in his *Munising Shipwrecks* expressed with eloquence the frustration of the sincere diver who found, on repeated visits to a wreck, the evidence of these underwater jackals.

Easily the most beautiful shipwreck in the Munising area is the *Smith Moore,* protected from excessive plundering by depth and location, though she has been largely stripped of small articles. Like all other wrecks, she had no interest in being where she is, but cruel fate intervened on July 13, 1889, when the nine-year-old vessel collided with the *James Pickands,* another freighter of the same length, 223 feet. Heavy fog aggravated the darkness, causing foghorns' blasts to elude analysis as to direction.

The *Pickands* arrived in Marquette at 9 a.m. the next day and reported the incident. Captain Ennis related striking the *Smith Moore* in a dense fog and recognizing her, but when no signals followed, he assumed no real damage was done. Little did he realize the plight of the *Smith Moore.*

Immediately after the impact Captain Morrison realized the collision had been a fatal blow to the *Smith Moore.* Some hours later, as the fog cleared, the steamer *M.M. Drake* sighted the *Moore* and came to her assistance. The crew and officers were taken off, and the *Smith Moore* was taken under tow toward Munising. She never arrived, sinking in the east channel near Trout Point. Her well-preserved remains lie in 105 feet of water.

The *Pickands* eventually paid the ultimate price for her part in the sinking of the *Moore.* In 1894 she laid her bones to rest on dreaded Sawtooth Reef at Eagle River, Michigan. In so doing, she joined at least 10 other wrecks, including the recently rediscovered *W.C. Moreland.*

Oddly enough, the cause of both of these ships' demise was the same: extensive forest fires had shrouded the lake in a smoky haze.

45

*Sketch of the* America *wreck.*

*The* America *, circa 1925.*

At 1:00 a.m. on the morning of June 7, 1928, the 180-foot steamer *America* docked at the Washington Club in Washington Harbor on the southwest end of Isle Royale. She was on her usual trip along the north shore between Duluth and the Canadian cities of Port Arthur and Fort William.

Her cargo unloaded, she backed away and proceeded to back out of Washington Harbor. In command was Mate Wick, who had taken over from Captain Edward Smith after the vessel got under way. It was a dark night, but visibility was not impaired by weather or fog. As the *America* turned into what is known locally as the North Gap, between the main island and Thompson Island, the center of the narrow channel was hidden in dark shadows. The *America* hit the sloping shoal bank of the main island, glancing away from the impact and continuing her course toward the open lake. It was after some 600 feet of water were under her keel that word came from the engine room that the pumps could not contain the rising water in the bilge.

Captain Smith appeared on the bridge in full uniform, glaring frostily at First Mate Wick. "Turn her around" was his command. The return trip held much danger since the darkness effectively concealed the entrance to the North Gap.

They found the gap, planning to beach the *America* in a shallow cove on the main island. Instead, they struck heavily on the same shoal as before. The force of impact drove her well up on the rocky bank, where, after a series of rolls both to port and starboard, she settled and sank. The only casualty was a dog, which was chained to the after deck. Plans to salvage the *America* were thwarted by extensive ice damage the following winter, and then by the Depression of 1929. [See detailed story on page 66].

**Left:** *Hallway of the* America *at 50 feet.* Photo by Jerry Eliason

*The Model A pickup truck on the* America.
Photo by Jerry Eliason

After over 50 years of damage, both from ice and from looters, the remains of the *America* lie in four to 85 feet of water. A serious attempt to refloat her was undertaken in 1966 [See story page 72] but this also met with failure. Even today, she remains one of the most visited wrecks on the lake.

For the sunken ships of Lake Superior, time stands still.  □

*"Now, gentlemen, in their interflowing aggregate, these grand fresh-water seas of ours — Erie and Ontario and Huron and Superior and Michigan — possess an ocean-like expansiveness. They contain round archipelagoes of romantic isles. They have heard the fleet thunderings of naval victories. They are swept by Borean and dismasting waves as direful as any that lash the salted wave. They know what shipwrecks are; for, out of sight of land, however inland, they have drowned many a midnight ship with all its shrieking crew."*

Ishmael in *Moby Dick*

# Diving the Lake

## *"All you have left are the photographs."*

FOR MOST OF US, TAKING a picture is as easy as pushing a button. For the divers of Lake Superior, this simple process is tinged with extra excitement, danger and technical problems.

The photographs on these pages were taken at depths of up to 240 feet. At that distance from the surface, normal rules of photography do not apply. Divers must guard against nitrogen narcosis (each 33 feet of descent is calculated to distort the senses roughly as much as drinking one martini), as well as debilitating cold (the water remains a chill 39 degrees Fahrenheit year-round).

The haunting *Gunilda* photographs were taken with an 80-pound camera, specially designed to float "neutral" in the water. Divers worked in eight-minute sessions, followed by 2½ hours of decompression time as they slowly rose to the surface. These precautions are vital; in recent years, this wreck has claimed the lives of five divers.

Many wrecks, however, are more accessible than the *Gunilda*, and most divers do not venture so dangerously deep. The pictures of the *Emperor*, for example, were taken at 150 feet. At this depth, longer dives are possible with considerably shorter decompression times. The pictures shown were shot with a normal 35mm camera, albeit protected by a Plexiglas housing.

Still, this is a deep dive, and divers must always exercise extreme care. Cut off from the surface, they must continually fight the narcotic effect of the "rapture of the deep." Breathing compressed air, the divers descend in dry suits with their gauges, timers and cameras. Visibility, and the quality of photographs, can be hampered by rain and wind on the surface, sandy or silty bottoms, warm or shallow water and algae.

Despite the difficulties, a visit to a wreck resting far down in the frigid darkness can yield benefits. In general, the deeper a wreck, the more intact it stays; heavy winter ice, often reaching down 70 feet, can break up ships lying near the surface. In addition, ships are less likely to be vandalized. Far from the natural light of the sun, photographs can be taken solely with strobe lights, simplifying film exposure.

The difficulties and rewards of underwater photography are too numerous for us to fully discuss here. Can we even ask the divers: "Why do you do it?" Obviously the rewards, some of which we have seen on the preceding pages, far exceed the difficulties.

At 240 feet, where the *Gunilda* lies, her cabin doors locked, her cabinets intact, the insidious influence of pressure nearly wins out. It is difficult to know what you're doing or what you did, said one diver. "All you have left are the photographs." *Tracy Biga*

48

**Opposite page:** *The* Edmund Fitzgerald *from the Elmer Engman Collection. Hand-tinted by Pam Davis.* **Left:** *The* Edmund Fitzgerald *was positively identified through a series of underwater pictures.* **Right:** *A cabin chair sits calmly on the deck of the* Fitzgerald. Spirit of the North Theatre Collection

by James R. Marshall

# The Edmund Fitzgerald Tragedy

AT about 7:20 p.m. on November 10th, 1975, Lake Superior swallowed the *Edmund Fitzgerald*, a giant 729-foot ore freighter. The lake was in the iron grip of an incredible storm, destined to be one of the worst in almost 30 years. Several other vessels were caught in the same general area, the *Arthur M. Anderson*, *Roger Blough* and the *Wilfred Sykes.*

The fact that the *Edmund Fitzgerald* should succumb to the violence of the lake while others made it to the refuge of Michigan's Whitefish Point is indeed a mystery, if one accepts the conclusions of the National Transportation Safety Board. Yet another point to ponder is that she carried an experienced crew and captain, men well versed in the operation of such a vessel under every condition found on the Great Lakes.

Except for the attention drawn to the wreck by an immensely popular song which appeared not long afterward, the *Fitzgerald* would have joined the *Carl D. Bradley,* which sank in 1958, and the *Daniel J. Morrell,* breaking up and sinking in 1966, in anonymity. These vessels also perished violently on the Great Lakes, but are now of interest only to historians and, of course, the shattered families whose lives were forever changed by their loss. One additional difference is apparent; both *Bradley* and *Morrell* had at least one survivor able to recount the dying moments of their proud ships. The *Fitzgerald* had only a mournful dirge to mark its violent and untimely passing.

Entombed within the battered wreckage, which lies in 530 feet of water, are the only real witnesses. Common sense dictates they had no chance to cry out for help; the flooding was immediate and total. For those in the pilothouse, it would have been the horrifying realization that the monster sea that was engulfing them was real. Through shattering windows, water was suddenly everywhere. It wasn't a wave entering, it was Lake Superior. For the balance of the crew, it can be assumed their last moments were full of shock and total surprise as the bone-chilling water sought them out in their various duty stations. Spreading from the now windowless pilothouse, it found stairways and passages, seeking to claim the prize it eventually won. The cascades of frenzied sea

49

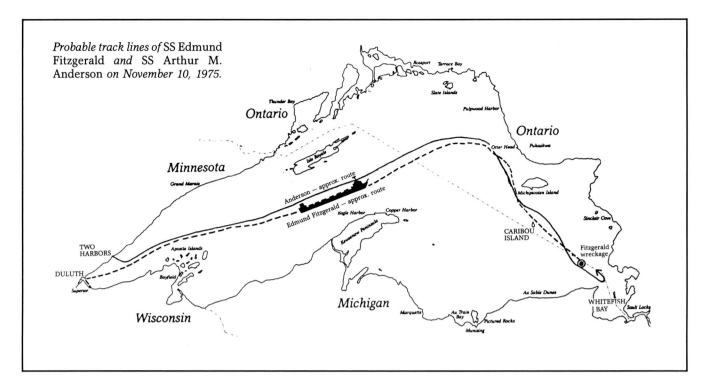

*Probable track lines of* SS Edmund Fitzgerald *and* SS Arthur M. Anderson *on November 10, 1975.*

### THE EDMUND FITZGERALD TRAGEDY

sought every nook and hiding place. The lake yielded only to the fast-moving mass of the ship itself as it submerged.

Probably the last noises heard by the crew during that shallow dive were a cacophony of tearing metal, unable to resist the surging tons of taconite cargo as it carried away bulkheads and burst hatches. Rushing water, shearing rivets and bursting portholes mixed with the muffled screams of fellow shipmates as they realized the hopelessness of their plight.

From sheer momentum the mud bottom almost swallowed the bow section of the *Fitzgerald.* She lies buried, close to her fully loaded line, in the timeless sediments which settled during the glacial epoch. The end probably came so quickly that no one suffered. Either concussion or pressure alone would have in-duced immediate unconsciousness.

The *Fitzgerald* was built at the River Rouge Works of the Great Lakes Engineering Company in 1958. She was officially No. 277437. Owned by the North-western Mutual Life Insurance Company of Milwaukee, she was

named for its president and chairman of the board and was christened by his wife.

The *Edmund Fitzgerald* entered the iron ore trade under charter to Oglebay Norton Company of Cleveland, Ohio, sailing under the colors of their Columbia Transportation Division. Until 1971, the *Fitzgerald* was the largest ship on the Great Lakes. Ironically, her successor to this title was the *Roger Blough,* the 850-foot U.S. Steel carrier laboring through the same storm on Lake Superior to the west of the *Fitzgerald* on November 10, 1975.

She was built to help meet a burgeoning demand for taconite pellets, found to be a superior blast-furnace feed in the steel industry. Northwestern Mutual invested in this new industry with the construction of the first taconite plant in Minnesota. The boat was a further expression of their solid belief in the future of steelmaking.

Aside from a few unplanned meetings with the piers at Sault Ste. Marie, the *Fitzgerald* suffered only two major incidents; one was a grounding at the Soo in 1969 and the other a collision with the

Canadian steamer *Hochelaga* in April 1970.

Twice she was reinforced in the keelson area, in 1969 and again in 1974. Ore boats have no external keel and the inner keelson also divides the ballast tanks. In 1969, a ''bow thruster'' was installed, a tube running crosswise in the lower bow containing a variable pitch propeller. This added greatly to maneuverability, and many of these devices were installed on lakers in those years. She was converted from coal to oil in 1972, with fuel tanks replacing her coal bunkers just forward from her after-cabin structure.

As befit her rank, the *Fitzgerald* was designed with guest quarters in the forward house, with accommodations and a small galley for four passengers. An elegant and spacious gathering room provided a view of the main, or ''spar,'' deck which stretched aft to the stern of the ship. Passengers were carried only during midsummer.

The *Edmund Fitzgerald* was indeed a proud vessel.

*continued on page 52*

*The* Irving S. Olds *twisting from the strain of a Great Lakes storm in 1972.* Photo from the Rus Hurt collection

# The Voyage

Captain Ernest M. McSorley was a veteran of the Great Lakes in every respect. He assumed command of the *Edmund Fitzgerald* in 1972, bringing his years of skilled vessel management and diplomatic personality to the bridge of the company flagship. Forty-four years of hard work, honing of native skills and persistence had paid off. Ernest McSorley in many ways was a "loner," but he had a warm and private side which only a chosen few knew. Next to the *Fitzgerald,* his invalid wife, Nellie, was his only other true love.

Leaving Superior, Wisconsin, on the afternoon of November 9 in beautiful weather, McSorley noted the forecast indicating that a strong weather system was approaching Lake Superior. What he did not know at that point was the strength of the impending "blow" and the effect it would soon have on the inland sea. Northeast winds with occasional periods of snow were forecast with waves of up to 15 feet. There was no question: It was November; the "scenic route" was the only course. This would take the *Fitzgerald* along the north shore of the lake, reducing somewhat the forces of the feared northeast waves.

As he passed Two Harbors, some 29 miles into the voyage, McSorley noted that the *Arthur M. Anderson* had departed from this port and was laying the same course. In conversations with Jesse Cooper, captain of the *Anderson,* it was agreed that the weather could be a problem and the northerly route would be the prudent course of action.

Paralleling the south shore of Isle Royale, the faster *Fitzgerald* had overtaken *Anderson,* one of U.S. Steel's larger vessels. [The *Anderson, Cason J. Calloway* and *Phillip R. Clark* were the "Queens" of the U.S. Steel Fleet.] Again, conversations between the two ships acknowledged the rapidly building seas, which by then were hurling themselves against the bows of both vessels. The barometer was dropping, as was the temperature. As predicted, the formerly decent weather was giving way to an increasing northeast sea. A heavy rain pelted the ship, reducing visibility. Waves were from the north-northeast, averaging 10 feet in height.

The *Fitzgerald* was a "Weather Ship," meaning she was one of

*Leaving Superior, Wisconsin, on the afternoon of November 9 in beautiful weather, McSorley noted the forecast indicating that a strong weather system was approaching Lake Superior. What he did not know at that point was the strength of the impending "blow" and the effect it would soon have on the inland sea.*

several vessels designated to regularly report weather conditions to the National Weather Service every six hours, or at any time if exceptional conditions warranted. At 1 a.m., November 10, the crew dutifully relayed the present environment, including the fact that winds were at 52 knots. This translates to 60 miles per hour. Later to be immortalized, the "Gales of November" had arrived.

Weather data from the *Fitzgerald* was meshed with other reports, generating a "Special Weather Bulletin" at 2 a.m. "Change gale warnings," it said, "to storm warnings, immediately." On the Great Lakes, this is the ultimate weather warning.

Now came additional weather information, this time indicating a rapid wind shift to the *NORTH-WEST* as the pressure cell moved across the lake. Just before 10 a.m. both vessels took up an easterly heading, seeking the shelter of the northern corner of the lake. With the Slate Islands, sentinels of the northeast corner clearly visible on the radar, both vessels began adjusting their courses to the southeast, to pass to the west of Michipicoten Island. By "cutting the corner," the *Anderson* moved closer to the *Fitzgerald,* reducing the distance between the ships to about eight miles. This placed the now reduced northeast sea on the port or left beam of the vessels, as both crews monitored the conditions which would foretell the impending wind switch.

Snow squalls obscured visibility as the rocky shore neared, but brief intervals of visibility revealed the revised wave pattern of a northwest sea, though the wind had subsided for the moment. *Fitzgerald* and *Anderson* were entering the "eye" of the storm.

Early afternoon found them clearing Michipicoten Island by three miles, with the faster *Fitzgerald* again increasing her lead. Courses were laid to pass to the south of this island and to the north of tiny Caribou Island, with its dreaded reef pattern which the charts clearly indicated reached out some five miles in a northerly direction. Another reef, "Chummy Bank," lay south of Michipicoten, necessitating a "thread the needle" course between the two shoal areas.

Mariners traveling this portion of Lake Superior had two charts available for their guidance in 1975. Since it was Canadian water, the primary chart was

Canadian Chart 2310, "Lake Superior, Caribou Island to Michipicoten Island," although vessels also carried the American Chart L.S. 9, which portrayed the entire lake, with some omission of detail. Both charts show the shoal area north of Caribou Island, known variously as Six Fathom Shoal and North Bank. Both charts were based on Canadian surveys made in 1916 and 1919 by the Canadian Hydrographic Service. [Though not pertinent to the *Fitzgerald* story, it is worthy to note that the dreaded "Superior Shoals," a large hump rising to within 21 feet of the surface of the lake some 82 miles east of Isle Royale, were not discovered until 1929 and were not shown on the maps.]

The American chart showed Six Fathom Shoal to be almost a half-mile east and a few hundred feet to the south of the location shown on the Canadian chart. In the early summer of 1976, some six months after the tragedy, the Canadian Hydrographic Survey found that both charts were terribly wrong. Another large shoal, which hovered only 24 feet below the surface, was discovered to be northeast of Caribou Island. Present-day charts reflect this expanded shoal area.

On that fateful day, with one set of radar out and the remaining radar a smaller set of limited scope, *Edmund Fitzgerald* was about to enter the 22-mile-wide channel between Michipicoten and Caribou Island.

The key to the successful transit of this confined area would obviously be knowing exactly where you were as you took up a planned heading to safely clear all hazards. Some masters trade a more severe beating for the safety of the deep water to the west of both islands, but they are in the minority. The habits of Great Lakes mariners usually take them between the islands. This might be the result of earlier experiences

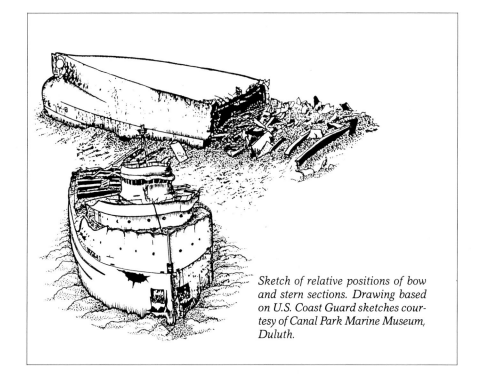

*Sketch of relative positions of bow and stern sections. Drawing based on U.S. Coast Guard sketches courtesy of Canal Park Marine Museum, Duluth.*

on smaller vessels, where being close to shore could enhance the chances of survival should something go wrong. Whatever the reason, both Ed McSorley of the *Fitzgerald* and "Bernie" Cooper of the *Anderson* chose the between-the-islands route. Cooper, however, decided to work to the west before going in, to assure that the now rapidly building seas would be to his stern.

Just before 2 p.m., Cooper advised McSorley of his plan, but McSorley elected to continue his almost due-south course, though he admitted he was "rolling some." As the *Anderson* moved to the west, the distance between the two ships increased from eight miles to about 17 when the *Fitzgerald* was entering the shoal area north of Caribou.

There was no reason for the *Anderson* to make note of the exact point at which the *Fitzgerald* altered her course to enter the passage. The turn to the southeast was made too late; the vessel was already farther to the south than they thought. The course of 141 degrees was intended to skirt Caribou Island by about five miles, well clear of the known shoals. The 24-foot bank, as yet

unknown to anyone, lay directly ahead. The late turn coupled with the increasingly violent seas combined to carry the *Fitzgerald* even closer to the known and dreaded Six Fathom Shoal. But invisible, just beneath the waves, the unknown shoal waited. In calm water it had a minimum depth of only 36 feet. The fully loaded *Fitzgerald* approaching in wildly surging seas was drawing 27 feet. In such conditions, she could easily have been set down on the shoal or, by chance, been partially carried over an even shallower one.

At about 3:30 p.m., the first mate on the *Anderson* asked Captain Cooper to look at the radar, which clearly indicated *Fitzgerald* was passing, in the mate's opinion, too close to the shoals of Caribou Island. The winds at this time were in excess of 40 knots, and snowfall quickly created blizzard conditions.

It was November, and it was clear from both reports and visual observations that a major storm was at hand. The skills of the crews of both *Anderson* and *Fitzgerald* were to be tested; but only one was destined to survive.

53

Captain Cooper studied the radar picture. The *Fitzgerald* was now some 16 miles ahead, crossing to the north of Caribou Island. "Closer," he was to later testify, "than I wanted the *Anderson* to be."

No longer able to run with the rapidly building seas, *Anderson* noted the wind to be 43 knots, with waves rapidly building and crashing at an angle from the stern across her deck. To gain such access required the seas to be in excess of 12 feet, and some were acknowledged to be about 16 feet in height. Ice was forming everywhere, adding to the torment already besetting the heavily laden vessels. Confined to the cabins by the weather, worried boatswains, we can assume, mentally recounted their last inspection of the hatches and other deck fittings.

Trouble of immense proportions found the *Fitzgerald* as she passed to the north of Caribou Island on a southeasterly course. The official findings of the Coast Guard refute her striking the shoal, but for the sake of conjecture, let us assume for the moment she did indeed find the shoal, which damaged her tanks to a fatal degree. With this assumption, the rest of the story falls into place.

Assume that the *Fitzgerald* "bottomed" north of Caribou Island. Very possibly, more than once. Those aboard, amid the din of high wind and rushing seas, might not have known it. In such sea conditions, pounding becomes an ever-present condition, hardly noted after a while if other problems preoccupy one's thoughts.

Assuming the grounding, the *Fitzgerald* would have "hogged," in the parlance of the lakes. Both the bow and the stern, not being supported by the shoal, would have bent downward, raising the mid or supported section. The first equipment to react would be the cable fences along the edge of the deck. They would tighten and finally fail from the strain. Whether the straining three strands of cable could have torn at or dislodged the tank vents is pure conjecture, not worthy of discussion beyond the comments made in Captain McSorley's next radio transmission.

By radio, Captain McSorley reported to *Anderson* that his ship had "a fence rail down, two vents damaged and a list." To mariners, a list means the vessel no longer

**Snow squalls obscured visibility as the rocky shore neared, but brief intervals of visibility revealed the revised wave pattern of a northwest sea, though the wind had subsided for the moment. Fitzgerald and Anderson were entering the "eye" of the storm.**

rides evenly, but leans to one side or the other. McSorley added that he would slow down, to allow the *Anderson* to catch up and keep track of her.

In response to Captain Cooper's question, McSorley acknowledged that he had his pumps going. "Yes," he said, "both of them."

An ore boat is really a long, somewhat divided cargo hold, surrounded on the bottom and part of the side by tanks. Such vessels must ride reasonably low in the water, both for stability and to provide a "bite" for the propeller. Loaded, this is no problem, but for the return or empty trip, the tanks must be partially flooded to increase the draft. Most vessels have many ballast tanks, fully divided, enabling the crew to "fine tune" the trim of the vessel to meet all sea conditions. Only on rare occasions is water allowed into the cargo hold itself, but drains leading to pumps are provided for just such an occasion. Otherwise, water levels are maintained in the various tanks or extracted by piping leading to, in the case of the *Fitzgerald*, six pumps. If the hold has a load of cargo, the pumps cannot drain the cargo hold, since the cargo obstructs the grates leading to the pumps, or "rose boxes" as they are known among mariners. The main purpose of the tanks is to sufficiently immerse the vessel that she might come alongside a loading dock and maintain a constant depth by adjusting the tank contents as cargo is loaded.

Witnesses being absent, we must make certain assumptions from what data is known. All such ships have "King Gauges" in the engine room, mercury devices which reflect the amount of water present in each tank. Chief Engineer George Holl would have known from a brief inspection just how the valves should be lined up to begin pumping the intruding water overboard. His tools were four 7,000-gallon-per-minute pumps in addition to two 2,000-gallon-per-minute pumps known as the "auxiliary pumps." Barring a hole in the skin of the vessel, these were more than adequate to handle just about any situation. Only one logical conclusion remains: when McSorley spoke of "both" pumps, he meant that he had started two pumps to remove water from the ballast tanks, *NOT THE CARGO HOLD.*

The crew of the *Anderson* made note of the damage report in their log but did not, in fact, fear for the safety of the *Fitzgerald*. Whether McSorley realized the extent of the damage will never be known, but in all probability he did. He advised Captain Cooper on the *Anderson* that he was "checking down" or slowing his vessel. "Will you," he asked, "stay by me until we get down?"

*Anderson* affirmed they would indeed assist in any way possible. Both captains knew that a new danger had been dealt into the game. In a sea which follows, speed becomes everything. Every wave tries to turn the ship into the trough of the waves, and speed alone gives the rudder the control necessary to fight this constant enemy. *Fitzgerald* was knowingly giving away part of her security, in trade for assistance, should it become necessary. Few vessels could survive broaching for any length of time in these seas. Most would be capsized or broken in two by such conditions, should they persist.

At about this time, the lock master at the Soo recorded winds in excess of 90 knots passing over the locks. Upon his orders, the Coast Guard broadcast a directive advising ships to seek safe shelter, adding that the locks were closed until further notice. Even the mighty Mackinac bridge was forced to close to highway traffic. Winds ranging from 75 to 82 knots were reported below the locks, with many vessels using power to maintain their anchored position.

Unseen by the crews of either vessel, the shrouded figure of Death, breathing the dank chill of impending demise, cast his hollow eyes about the expanse of tortured water, seeking victims. The *Fitzgerald*, imperceptibly settling deeper at the bow as water gained on the pumps, drew Death's rapt attention.

Whether Captain McSorley knew he had "bottomed" the *Fitzgerald* north of Caribou Island is of no real consequence. Even if he had suspected the damage, pride, plus a full belief and confidence in his ship, would

have precluded admitting such an error. Seasoned mariners just do not do such a thing unless the ship is in immediate peril. We can assume McSorley did not feel mortally wounded.

It could have been imagination. Was it really taking more time for the *Fitzgerald* to recover from the onslaught of each major wave?

It is normal practice when a ship develops a list to add water to tanks on the opposite side. This is done for several reasons. The

*Assuming the grounding, the Fitzgerald would have "hogged", in the parlance of the lakes. Both the bow and the stern, not being supported by the shoal, would have bent downward, raising the mid or supported section. The first equipment to react would be the cable fences along the edge of the deck.*

suction to drain the tanks is near the centerline of the ship, so with a list the tank cannot be completely emptied. A list greatly affects the steering, causing the ship to take longer to respond to the rudder. Water is placed in the opposite tanks, since this creates the least strain on the structure of the hull, but the rule is pump first, add water only as a last resort. Only a few seasoned skippers will add water at the other end of the vessel on the opposite side to the list. The strain is traded for trim, keeping the vessel level from bow to stern,

assisting both in propulsion and steering. Just where, or even if, Captain McSorley did try to trim his ship will never be known.

One thing was certain: Both of the *Edmund Fitzgerald's* radars had ceased functioning. As they left the meager shelter of Caribou Island, McSorley needed help, and he radioed *Arthur M. Anderson*, "I've lost both radars; can you assist me in navigation?" *Anderson* quickly agreed. The time was then 4:10 p.m. on November 10. The *Fitzgerald* had about three hours left to live. Unfortunately, no person was then aware of the various problems and the effect of the catastrophic weather, except a very few in the pilothouse of the stricken ship.

[The final Coast Guard report dismissed the possibility of the grounding on Caribou Island shoal. It even discusses a "large floating object" as a likely possibility to account for the damage and subsequent loss. One can but wonder just what "large floating object" might have been loose on the lake that night that would disable and sink a 729-foot ore boat. The Coast Guard also decided that "improper hatch clamps" might have either not been in place or failed, allowing large volumes of water into the cargo hold. This convoluted theory fails in one prime analysis: Had the cargo hold been flooding, as the Coast Guard postulates, why use the pumps? No list would have been apparent and, in such seas, settling in the water would not have been measurable.]

Clearing the confused seas south and east of Caribou, the *Fitzgerald's* next safety lay in the lee of Whitefish Point. McSorley had run out of options; this was his only choice. His tenuous understanding of his position lay in the radar bearings reported by the *Anderson*, still miles astern coping with the same conditions. The *Anderson* did advise that some traffic was upbound ahead of him, three "salties," or foreign ships, just clearing Whitefish. McSorley was told he would steer clear of them easily.

The *Fitzgerald*'s only tool left to aid in navigation was the Radio Direction Finder, which could be used for determining the bearing to the Whitefish Point Lighthouse. This station, normally both a distinctive light and a radio beacon, had been converted from a manned station to a "remote" in 1975. Supposedly fully automated, it provided McSorley but one brief signal, then nothing.

Aboard the leading salty, the Swedish ship *Avafors,* Captain Cedric Woodard, serving as a Great Lakes pilot, responded to a radio call to "any vessel in the vicinity of Whitefish Point." It was the *Edmund Fitzgerald,* downbound.

Not recognizing the voice, Woodard asked to whom he was speaking. "This," said the strange voice "is Captain McSorley."

Captain Woodard had known McSorley for many years and had often spoken to him. "I didn't recognize your voice," he replied. Immediate concern flooded his thoughts; something was wrong.

McSorley wanted to know if either the light or radio beacon was working at Whitefish Point. Woodard had to tell him that neither was. McSorley had lost his last means of knowing his exact course to safety. If the radios failed, preventing guidance from *Anderson,* he was doomed.

That corner of the lake is treacherous at any time; its infamous Pancake Shoal had claimed many ships in similar conditions. The shoal lay, he thought, somewhat to the left and just a few miles ahead. Now the backside of the storm was reaching its height. Winds were averaging 72 knots, gusting to 84 knots (over 96 miles per hour), and waves were approaching 30 feet. Woodard would later testify, "It was one of the biggest seas I

have ever been in."

Some three miles behind *Avafors* was *Benfri,* piloted by Captain Robert O'Brien. Another two miles behind was a third vessel, *Nanfri,* piloted by veteran Captain Albert Jacovetti. Both pilots echoed Woodard's remarks.

At about 5:30 p.m., the sudden flash of Whitefish Light startled Woodard, just to his left. He immediately advised the *Fitzgerald* that it was working, though no radio beacon signal was received. McSorley replied with understatement, "I'm very glad to hear it."

Not wanting to terminate the conversation, Woodard added, "It's really howling down here. What are the conditions like up where you are?"

"We are taking heavy seas over our decks," he replied. "It's the worst sea I have ever been in. We have a bad list and no radar."

Woodard said he thought the *Fitzgerald* had two radars. Woodard asked, "Are they both out?"

"Yes," McSorley replied, "both of them."

The *Fitzgerald* had one large radar antenna, which could be used by either of two identical receivers. Later examination of the wreckage revealed that the radar mast was missing.

The *Fitzgerald* was steadily losing her ability to cope with the incredible seas. With each assaulting monster wave, her bow settled imperceptibly, unable to recover before the next attack.

On the *Anderson,* First Mate Morgan Clark called the *Fitzgerald.* His concern was the course *Fitzgerald* seemed to be holding, since on the radar she seemed to be moving to the left. The time was 6:20 p.m. Had gyrocompass problems been added to the frustrating loss of both radars?

"We are steering 141," was the reply. Clark was concerned. This was the same heading as the

*Anderson,* but radar confirmed it was not the actual course of the *Fitzgerald.*

At 7 p.m. Clark advised they had Crisp Point, some 12 miles west of Whitefish, on the radar at 25 miles. "You are 15 miles from Crisp Point." He added, "We haven't got far to go; we will soon have it made." McSorley agreed.

"It's a hell of a night for the Whitefish beacon not to be operating," Clark observed.

Again, McSorley agreed.

At about 7:10, First Mate Clark noted a vessel moving out of Whitefish Bay and advised the *Fitzgerald* they had a vessel nine miles ahead but would clear it without a problem. Out of genuine concern, Clark asked, "By the way, how are you making out with your problem?"

"We are," McSorley replied, "holding our own."

Signing off, First Mate Morgan Clark was unaware he had just heard the last transmission ever to be made by the *Edmund Fitzgerald.* Her now unavoidable appointment with the depths of Lake Superior was but moments away. No power or force could save her.

Captain Cooper had been briefly absent from the pilothouse of the *Anderson* during this last exchange. Returning, he watched the *Fitzgerald* sail into a "white blob" of sea echo on the radar. Blinding snow surrounded the *Anderson;* visibility was near zero. At about 7:25 p.m., he would later testify, the snow stopped, revealing the lights of the *Avafors, Benfri* and *Nanfri,* all upbound from Whitefish Bay. The lights of the *Fitzgerald* should be much closer, but they just were not there!

Repeated radio calls brought no response. No target, except intermittent echoes at eight miles, appeared on the radar. Had her electrical circuits somehow failed she should still appear on the radar. The unthinkable, horrifying

one on the stern and one on the bow. Such devices are designed to float free of a sinking vessel and to inflate automatically. Both were found in an inflated condition, but empty.

The remains of the life boats were picked up by the *William R. Roesch* and *James D.* The boats and the rafts were taken to the Coast Guard station at the Soo for inspection. As might be supposed, the lifeboats showed no evidence of an attempt to launch them. One lifeboat is on display at the Soo Marine Museum, aboard the *Valley Camp,* an ore freighter on permanent display at that facility.

On November 14, the first in a long series of underwater search and survey efforts was begun. Using "Side Scan" sonar, a sophisticated type of underwater survey equipment which was installed aboard the *Woodrush* for the search, wreckage was found on the first day. It was later determined to be the *Fitzgerald.* As the search continued, two objects were outlined, lying in close proximity in 530 feet of water, each approximately 300 feet in length. A "roughened" area between them was thought to be cargo. The sonar equipment was found to be inadequate for such depth and was hampered further by recurrent bad weather. The Marine Board suggested that a second and more thorough search be conducted, using a commercial contractor, Seaward, Inc., of Falls Church, Virginia.

Again using *Woodrush* as a platform, the second search commenced on November 22, in extremely bad weather. Over a three-day period some 80 runs were made, generating some 300 navigational fixes. This effort was put forth to gather the maximum amount of data, which was carefully analyzed at the contractor's facility. A model of the wreckage was constructed, reflecting the best guesses at what was really down there, as interpreted from the extensive search data.

Based on this exhaustive effort, the Marine Board concluded that the wreckage was "very probably that of the *Fitzgerald.*" Since a means to visually inspect the site was available, it was recommended that it be employed.

*Captain Jesse Cooper and the crew of his* Arthur M. Anderson *had responded to the highest calling of the maritime occupation. To turn around was bad enough, risking the vessel's being trapped in the trough of those violent seas, but to do so knowing that at least ONE MORE TURN must be made out there, where the* Anderson *might well succumb to the same strains that might have taken the* Fitzgerald, *took extreme courage.*

The report concluded that the wreckage formed a "Vee," but the possibility existed that it might be two ships.

Dr. Julius F. Wolff, then a professor at the University of Minnesota, Duluth, was consulted. Known and respected leading authority on Lake Superior shipwrecks, Dr. Wolff agreed that another ship might lie in the position indicated. "Many ships," he pointed out, "are 'just missing' in eastern Lake Superior, having never been found."

Arrangements were made to visually inspect the site. Again, the *Woodrush* served as the "mother" ship for this search.

Beginning on May 12, 1976, a third Side Scan sonar survey was initiated. The results essentially mirrored the earlier inspection. This time, however, anchor locations were determined, to stabilize *Woodrush* during the final inspection. It would utilize the U.S. Navy CURV III (Controlled Underwater Recovery Vehicle), the same device used to recover a nuclear weapon from 2,800 feet of water off the coast of Spain some years earlier.

CURV III is tethered to a surface support vessel by power and other cables allowing it to be maneuvered from the surface. It consists of a frame approximately six by 15 feet mounted on two horizontal propulsion motors, one vertical propulsion motor, lights, a 35mm camera, two black-and-white TV cameras and a controllable arm. The vehicle operates on power supplied by generators installed on the support vessel and is operated by a control van, also placed aboard the support vessel. Videotape recording equipment, sonar recording and position determination instruments are also fitted into the van. The CURV III was the "tool for the job" and would soon answer many questions.

It must be understood that at this moment, before the CURV III descended into the shadowy depths, no one really knew if the target was the *Fitzgerald,* or what condition the wreck was in.

It was indeed the *Fitz,* in two pieces, torn asunder by forces almost unknown to living beings.□

*Captain Jesse B. Cooper*

# SS *Arthur M. Anderson:* November 10, 1975

## *The last ship to see the* Fitzgerald

**by Captain Jesse B. Cooper, Retired**

THE *ARTHUR M. ANDER-SON* departed Two Harbors, Minnesota, on the afternoon of November 9, 1975, one of the special days on Lake Superior — just ripples on the water — sunny and warm for November.

We could see the *Edmund Fitzgerald* about 10 miles astern.

Shortly after we left, the weather people put up small craft warnings. By the 6 p.m. weather report, they hoisted northeast gale warnings.

As is our policy, when the meteorologists become nervous we start our own weather plots. A low pressure to the south did show on our weather plots, but it really didn't

look as if it would become very drastic, just normal November low pressure.

As we continued east on our run to the Soo, both the *Fitz* and *Anderson* held to the north a few miles off Isle Royale.

At this time we were having a fringe gale — 30 to 35 knots, taking spray but with no green water on deck. The *Fitz,* being a faster ship, overtook us off Isle Royale.

Our midnight weather plot gave us the low's direction of movement. It should pass over the Marquette area. Though there was no sign of deepening, we were still having the northeast winds, being on the front

side of the low pressure. It now appeared to us that we would be on the back side of the low during the last part of our run to Whitefish Bay — with winds over the stern.

As we approached Michipicoten Island, the low had reached Lake Superior and was intensifying dramatically. The weather plot told us to expect 80-knot winds on the back side. Still, the wind and sea would be astern. We should still make out okay.

Shortly after noon on the 10th, we were in the eye of the storm. The sun was out; light winds, no sea.

The *Fitz* at this time was north and east of the *Anderson.* She stayed on the northeasterly course while we in effect cut a corner. We hauled for a position two miles off Michipicoten's west end. Meanwhile the *Fitz* had passed the west end lighthouse. As we approached Michipicoten, the wind shifted to the west-northwest, and we started to roll. There was a dead swell from the southwest. We hauled a bit to counter the roll for a few miles, then hauled back for a position of six miles off the northeast tip of Caribou Island, a course of 120 degrees true.

The *Fitzgerald* was to the east of us, a fact which raises certain questions: What was her course, 150 degrees? Possibly to take her in closer to Caribou Island to get what benefit she could of the lee?

As we intersected that 141-degree course for the Bay, we noted by the heading flasher on the radar that the *Fitz* was to the west of our course line. She was maybe too close to Caribou Island.

Prior to this the last time we saw the *Fitz* was off the Michipicoten west end as it had started to snow. From this point on all the fixes [and sightings] were by radar.

The time was 1520 [3:20 p.m.]. The *Fitzgerald* called with the info that she had a fence rail down and two vents damaged plus a starboard list. He [Captain Ernest M. McSorley] also had his pumps going so that means that the *Fitz* had to have water in one or two of her side tanks. Possibly a stress fracture of the hull.

At this time the *Fitz* was mortally wounded. How bad we wouldn't know until later. My own opinion is that she bottomed out on a shoal. This area had not been surveyed since the 1915 era.

The wind and sea were increasing rapidly. The sea was running 10 to 16 feet, west-northwest to northwest, 40 to 45 knots. We were taking green water on deck.

The *Fitz* again called. Her radars were out. She asked us to plot her position. We were running plots every half hour, and we marked her position and ours on the chart. This is a simple problem. You take a bearing on radar of a known object or point of land, run the oscar out [mileage gauge], bring the bearing back to true and lay it out on the chart. You then have a fix. We used our fix and projected the *Fitz* bearings the same way to give her a position.

We cleared the south end of Caribou. The seas were very large, 25 to 35 feet. We were now taking a lot of water on deck, as much as 12 feet. Sometime before 7 p.m. we took two of the largest seas of the trip. The first one flooded our boat deck. It had enough force to come down on the starboard lifeboat, pushing it into the saddles with a force strong enough to damage the bottom of the lifeboat.

The first mate, Morgan Clark, on his way back to the wheelhouse, stopped in each hold to check on our watertight integrity. All was well. Just a bit of condensation. The *Fitz* and the *Anderson* have identical hatch fasteners.

The second large sea put green water on our bridge deck! This is about 35 feet above the waterline!

More questions: Did these two large seas reach the *Fitzgerald* at 7:10 p.m.? With a following sea? Green water boarding a ship will stay on deck for a longer period of time. It would, with the increased weight of the water, increase the draft of the ship by a considerable amount.

Morgan Clark had contact with the *Fitz* at 7:10 p.m.

I somehow believe these large seas joined up forward of the *Fitz*. They nosed her down, which then started her plunge to the bottom. Viewing the underwater pictures, I feel it is evident that she hit a mountain on the bottom of the lake. Pictures showed many holes in her bow. If this is true, when she hit the bottom, she collapsed in the middle like an accordion. The pictures showed 200 feet to be missing. She could well have torn at the area of the previous damage.

Our radars were not able to receive a clear picture close in, due to the large seas which were returning an echo to our scopes.

The *Fitz* was entering this phenomenon on our scope eight to nine miles ahead and to port.

A short time later [a half hour?] the snow cleared. We could see the vessels outbound from Whitefish Bay. We tried to locate the *Fitz* by phone and ships in the vicinity.

The first mate and I were at this time working both radars, using the suppressors to try to get a target. We did think at one time that we did have a faint target. It was beginning to be a grim reality that the *Fitz* was gone.

We proceeded into Whitefish Bay, and with a partial lee from Parisienne Island we turned around and headed back to the suspected area.

Strange as it may seem, we had a real gung-ho sailor aft who wanted to be in a "Real Storm." He was informed by the chief engineer that we were turning around and heading back out. He went to his room, broke out the tape recorder, gave his last will and testament, sealed it in wax and put it in a jar so the world would know what happened to the *Anderson!*

After we turned, we laid out a course from our last known position of the *Fitz,* west-northwest of an area clear of all the shoals in the area. When we reached this line, we headed into the wind, hoping to find some people.

The issue of turning was not without doubts among the ship's crew. What could we do if we found some of the *Fitz* crew?

At 5:30 a.m. we encountered debris: oars, life jackets, ring buoys, gas cylinders.

My crew manned the search light and flood lights throughout the whole ordeal. I could not have had a better group of people if I had hand picked them myself.

A few things have changed because of the *Fitzgerald* tragedy. Strobe lights are now required on life jackets and ring buoys. Also, survival suits have been developed, plus a new type of unsinkable capsule is a possibility. □

The power of Lake Superior is graphically shown through the damage to the Edmund Fitzgerald's cabin. Debris from the wreck is abundant as shown in the photographs from the CURV III vehicle.
**Below:** Wreckage from the Edmund Fitzgerald *found floating in Lake Superior.*

# The Fitzgerald Board Report
## *The reasons were many, but inconclusive*

**by Dr. Julius F. Wolff, Jr.**　　　　**photos courtesy of Canal Park Marine Museum**

More than a decade has elapsed since the giant taconite carrier *Edmund Fitzgerald* vanished northeast of Whitefish Point on the evening of November 10, 1975, taking her crew of 29 to eternity. Despite an intensive Coast Guard investigation, an official Coast Guard report on the sinking and a counter report by the Lake Carriers Association, opinions and theories on the cause of sinking continue to blossom forth. Seldom has a Lake Superior shipwreck attracted more public attention. Indeed, the sinking of the "Big Fitz" involved the worst property loss in the history of Lake Superior sailing, while the death toll of 29 places this incident among the top 10 fatal shipwrecks on this lake.

After two and a half years of detailed study, the National Transportation Safety Board attempted to place all known facts on the *Fitzgerald* disaster in perspective. Their study, *Marine Accident Report: SS* Edmund Fitzgerald *Sinking in Lake*

*Superior, November 10, 1975* (Report Number NTSB-MAR-78-3), presented a succinct analysis of innumerable relevant factors: the construction, operational and inspection history of the ship, professional backgrounds of the officers, a continuous travelogue of the fatal voyage, the highly significant observations of officers controlling the trailing SS *Arthur M. Anderson,* the periodic weather bulletins of the National Weather Service, results of the search and rescue attempts of the Coast Guard, Navy and private carriers, together with a minute examination of the on-the-bottom findings in May 1976 by the Coast Guard task force utilizing the CURV III vehicle mothered by the Coast Guard cutter *Woodrush.*

The CURV III device made 12 dives into 530 feet of water, logged 56 hours and 5 minutes of bottom time, made 43,255 feet of videotape with its television camera, plus 985 still color photographs. After view-

ing this mass of evidence and thousands of pages of testimony, the National Transportation Safety Board by a 3-1 decision concluded that the abrupt demise of the *Fitzgerald* was caused by sudden, massive flooding of the cargo hold due to the collapse of one or more hatch covers under giant boarding seas. This was made possible by a gradual loss of freeboard over a period of hours through leakage resulting from deck damage or dented hatch coamings. Chair James B. King was joined by members Francis H. McAdams and Elwood T. Driver in the majority decision, but member Philip A. Hogue vigorously dissented, alleging that the quantity of water necessary to overcome the 14,000-gallons-a-minute forward pumps and cause reduced freeboard could only have come from a holing of the hull through shoaling as the ship rounded the northeast corner of Caribou Island, four hours prior to the catastrophe.

Built in 1958 by the Great Lakes Engineering Works, River Rouge, Michigan, Hull No. 301, the *Edmund Fitzgerald* was a conventional "straight deck" Great Lakes bulk carrier, 729 feet overall, with a width of 75 feet and a depth of 39 feet. Her gross tonnage was 13,612, net tonnage 8,686. Her steam turbine power plant generated 7,500 horsepower. A diesel-driven bow thruster was added in 1969, and in 1972 her fuel system was converted from coal to oil. Her cargo hold measured 860,950 cubic feet, divided by two (non-watertight) screen bulkheads. Outboard of the hold were eight ballast tanks; above these were two tunnels leading from stem to stern for travel by the crew in rough weather. The hold possessed 12 hatch openings 11 x 48 feet, with hatch coamings extending 24 inches above the weather deck. Hatch covers were 5/16-inch stiffened steel plates, weighing 14,000 pounds, with a 9/16th-inch rubber gasket around the underside perimeter of each. These were removed and replaced by a traveling deck crane. Each hatch cover was secured by 68 manually operated "Kestner" clamps spaced on two-foot centers.

Protruding 18 inches above the weather deck were two eight-inch vent pipes for each of the ballast tanks. The ship was fitted with four 7,000-gallons-per-minute main pumps and two 2,000-gallons-per-minute auxiliary pumps. She also possessed a variety of radios, some on ship's power and others on batteries for emergency. Altogether, the *Edmund Fitzgerald* was a well-constructed, extensively equipped modern freighter.

The ship was authorized to carry 49 persons. Hence, lifesaving equipment included two 50-person lifeboats located starboard and port side on the stern, two 25-person self-inflating life rafts, one at the bow and one on the stern, 24 life rings and 83 life preservers. Lifeboats presumably could be launched in 10 minutes. The crew had participated in 14 fire and boat drills during the 1975 navigation season.

During her 17 years of operation the *Fitz* had an excellent record. She had sustained one grounding, was involved in a slight collision and several times had struck lock walls. During a major overhaul in 1969 some minor cracking was detected and corrected. At her last drydocking at Cleveland in 1974 several lesser defects were remedied. In April 1975 she had been inspected by both the Coast Guard and the American Bureau of Shipping and found sound. Also, on October 31, 1975, a spot Coast Guard inspection had detected a few flaws around hatch coamings — dents or cracks probably caused by unloading equipment — but nothing of serious consequence.

The *Fitzgerald* was manned by a veteran crew. Captain Ernest M. McSorley had been a captain for 38 years and had sailed for 44 years. His first mate was likewise a captain for 34 years. Both held master's and first class pilot's licenses for ships of any tonnage on the Great Lakes. The second and third mates also had first class pilot's licenses. The chief engineer and four assistant engineers were likewise experienced officers. Twenty of the crew were unlicensed personnel.

Owner of the *Fitz* was the Northwestern Mutual Life Insurance Company, but she had been chartered to the Columbia Transportation Division of Oglebay-Norton Company, operators of a fleet of bulk carriers.

*The CURV III device made 12 dives into 530 feet of water, logged 56 hours and 5 minutes of bottom time, made 43,255 feet of videotape with its television camera, plus 985 still color photographs.*

## Investigation Results

Why did the *Fitzgerald* go down while lesser ships survived? A battery of experts examined the findings — representatives of the Coast Guard Marine Board of Investigation, the National Transportation Safety Board, the U.S. Navy Supervisor of Salvage, the Naval Undersea Center and the engineering consultant firm Seaward, Inc., which specialized in the electronic search and is under contract to the Navy Supervisor of Salvage.

The underwater evidence did not disclose why the *Fitzgerald* sank, but it did eliminate a number of potential explanations. Discounted were theories that the *Fitzgerald* broke in two on the surface through hull failure or that cargo shifted and she capsized. The bow section contained hatches 1 through 8. The hatch cover of No. 1 could be seen dropped into the hold. Hatch covers Nos. 3 and 4 apparently were in place, hatch cover No. 6 on edge but over the hold. Had the ship separated on the surface, the portions on the bottom would not be so closely juxtaposed, while if the vessel capsized, all hatch covers should have been blown out by the pressure of the cargo. Also, in capsizing, the whole vessel should be on its side or inverted, which was definitely not the case. The experts thus concluded that through the progressive flooding, because of hull injury sustained hours previously, the ship was slowly settling by the bow, though in the tremendous seas this was not apparent to the captain and officers. Then, with progressive boarding seas running the full length of the ship, such a head of water was built up over the forward hatches that some hatch covers collapsed, allowing more water in an already saturated hold so that the bow-heavy vessel simply buried its nose at the base of a giant wave and headed for the bottom. Striking at an angle in 530 feet of water with the stern unsupported, the stern section could wrench off and capsize while much of the middle cargo segment could simply disintegrate, which apparently was the situation. The end came so quickly that the pilothouse crew had no chance to sound a "Mayday" or, obviously, to call an "abandon ship." The crew must have been entombed within their ship, since, as far as is known, no body has ever been recovered.

Members of the National Transportation Safety Board were greatly concerned about the source of leakage on the *Fitzgerald*. Water obviously was entering the ship at a rate greater than her 32,000-gallons-per-minute total pumping capacity. Apparently, some hull damage had already occurred by 1530 hours, November 10, when Captain McSorley reported two vent tops gone, railing washed away and a list. He did not specify the cause of the damage, but the panel, noting that neither the deck crane nor spare propeller blade appeared in the wreckage, surmised that either or both might have broken loose to cause damage to the deck plates before going over the side. Something was awry on deck after 1700 hours, as Captain Cedric Woodard of the *Avafors* heard Captain McSorley interrupt their radio conversation to order "Nobody allowed on deck!" Of course, some large piece of debris might have been washed on board to cause injury. (The author has seen some enormous pieces of wood flotsam on the beaches west of Whitefish Point and on the eastern Canadian shore.) At any rate, ruptured deck plating must have been admitting water to the tunnels or to the hold.

The panel also suspected that the hatch covers of the *Fitz* were not watertight. The underwater pictures disclosed that a surprising number of the "Kestner" clamps on the hatch coamings had snapped open, indicating that they had not been properly set. The NTSB members calculated that a pressure of 178,000 pounds was required to make a hatch cover watertight; because the cover weighed only 14,000 pounds, the clamps would have had to be adjusted to provide the rest, and this did not appear to have been done. Likewise, when leaving her Superior dock, the *Fitzgerald* had been loaded to her maximum winter freeboard standard, namely, 11 feet, 6 inches. But she had been encountering waves 15 to 25 feet in height for many hours. Under such conditions, with depths of water up to 14 feet on deck, the insecure hatch covers must have been admitting steady quantities of water into the cargo hold well prior to the hatch cover collapse which marked the end. The captain would have no way of detecting this, as he had no instruments to check the trim and tilt while the ship was under way.

The Safety Board members spent a great deal of time analyzing evidence for the common belief that the *Fitzgerald* had shoaled north of Caribou Island. Captain Jesse Cooper of the *Anderson* had communicated his suspicion of shoaling in a taped radio message to his company after the *Fitz* had disappeared. At the Coast Guard hearing he had repeated this suspicion. Accordingly, the panel carefully plotted the courses of the *Fitzgerald* and *Anderson* from notations in the *Anderson* log for several hours before the sinking.

The *Anderson* had been using the National Oceanic and Atmospheric Agency Lake Survey Chart No. 9, "Lake Superior," Canadian Chart 2310, "Lake Superior, Caribou Island to Michipicoten Island" and NOAA Lake Survey Chart No. 92, "Lake Superior, St. Mary's River to Au Sable Point." While not all radar sightings and course changes had been recorded by *Anderson* officers on that stormy afternoon, the panel concluded from available course information that the *Fitzgerald* had not come within several miles of an area where she might have touched bottom. A resurvey in 1976 by the Canadian Hydrographic Service indicated that a six-fathom area on Chart No. 9 actually did not exist; in addition, the 1976 resurvey confirmed all essential data on Chart 2310, which had been based upon soundings obtained in 1919. Furthermore, an underwater survey by the Columbia Transportation Division in 1976 substantiated the information of the Canadian chart. Three of the National Transportation Safety Board members concluded that the *Fitzgerald* could not have holed herself on the bottom, but member Hogue would not agree, relying on Captain Cooper's initial assumptions. Pictures of the stern hull bottom disclosed no evidence of striking and showed the propeller and rudder to be undamaged.

The National Transportation Safety Board derived 18 conclusions from its investigation and presented 23 recommendations to the Coast Guard, the American Bureau of Shipping and the National Oceanic and Atmospheric Administration. Among the points stressed was the improvement of hatch covers and clamp mechanisms to insure that hatches are watertight. The Coast Guard was asked to step up its inspections of hatch closing procedures and to halt the departure of ships found delinquent. The Board also wondered if the reduction of minimum freeboard requirements in 1969, 1971 and 1973 constituted a safety hazard to the ships.

Greater attention to loading procedures was urged so that masters could take on cargo and pump out ballast without straining the hulls. The Board suggested the development of instruments to inform a master of water levels in the cargo holds, and also to detect changes in trim and heel. A fathometer would be useful in certain waters.

The Board urged that ships be required to carry Emergency Position Indicating Radio Beacons (EPIRB) so that an immediate location of a sunken vessel could be provided to assist rescue craft in finding survivors. In addition, the inadequate rescue capability of the Coast Guard in heavy weather was noted and improved equipment advised. The American Bureau of Shipping was asked to ascertain the limiting sea conditions for lakes vessels so that masters could avoid endangering their ships when such situations were imminent. More careful records should be kept of any mishaps which might weaken hull structure.

Finally, the National Oceanic and Atmospheric Administration was asked to improve and update the information on Chart No. 9 relative to the vicinity of Caribou Island, while NOAA's National Weather Service was asked to revise its method of estimating projected wave heights in storm periods. The bulletins of the Weather Service concerning wind direction in the *Fitzgerald* storm had been rather accurate, but estimates of wave heights had been up to 60 percent low.

Despite the careful investigations and studies, we still do not know exactly what factor or cluster of factors sank the *Edmund Fitzgerald,* but out of this tragedy have emerged increased precautions or practices which should mean a greater degree of ship safety on the lakes. □

*Reprinted from* The Nor'Easter *[January-February 1980], the journal of the Lake Superior Marine Museum Association.*

# LORAN — A Legacy of the Edmund Fitzgerald

After losing his radars, the captain of the *Edmund Fitzgerald* could only estimate where he really was on that stormy evening in 1975. In 1979, an additional LORAN station (Long Range Aid to Navigation) was commissioned at Baudette, Minnesota. This additional station brought an umbrella of information to western Great Lakes pilots: accurate position location, course being steered and speed. Long a standard navigation tool on the world's oceans, it was not deemed necessary on the lakes until the *Fitzgerald* tragedy.

Three stations, one in New York, one in Indiana and the Baudette station, all transmit a simultaneous signal. A small shipboard receiver measures the time delay difference between the two strongest station signals, instantly translating them to latitude and longitude. This data is displayed on an illuminated dial on the receiver, which is actually a small computer. As the rate of change is noted, it will also display speed, course made good and time-to-go to the next navigation point.

Now available to any boater with a spare $500, the newest LORAN receivers are no bigger than a cake-mix box. By storing a location as a "waypoint" in the receiver, a boater may return to within 50 feet of the same spot at any time.

Captain Mark Gainey of the Ford fleet was an early Lake Superior LORAN enthusiast. On one trip he and his shipmates were dumbfounded to find that a current, previously unknown, had moved their ore boat almost five miles laterally during their passage from Duluth to Sault Ste. Marie.

LORAN has made travel safer on our Great Lakes.

# The America

## *Memories of a friend*

by Thomas Holden

**Left:** *The America backing away from the dock. The four open loading gangways denote the ship after being lengthened in 1911. Early photos show only three. Captain Smith is just in front of the pilothouse. America's informality is evident with passengers even on the pilothouse.* **Above:** *The morning after the sinking. The bell, searchlight and wheel were removed by vandals just days after this photo was taken.* Elmer Engman Collection

**F**EW SHIPS THAT EVER sailed the Great Lakes could evoke fond memories like those held by north shore residents for a little passenger and package freighter that sailed between Duluth-Superior and Thunder Bay during the early 1900s.

She was the steamer *America* — a welcome and familiar visitor to all points along the shore, delivering passengers, mail and other goods from 1902 until 1928. Residents lost a friend in June 1928 when the *America* hit a reef off Isle Royale, Michigan, was beached and, ultimately, victimized by Lake Superior.

*A passenger cabin sink, one of the few remaining on the* America. *By pinching the "rabbit ears" on the faucet together, water would flow.* Photo by Bruce Bisping

*Captain Jacob Frederick Hector and the* America *made their rounds on time, despite Lake Superior's most treacherous weather and a rugged shoreline route.*

Ironically, the vessel is still a favorite among north shore visitors. Lying at a 45-degree angle with her bow only four feet below the surface, she is one of the most diveable among the 10 major shipwrecks in Isle Royale National Park. [See story, page 90.]

The *America* came to life in 1898 at the Detroit Dry Dock Company shipyard in Wyandotte, Michigan. The steel-hulled, single-bottom, single-screw steamer was powered by a 700 horsepower, triple expansion engine. She measured 164 feet in length, with a beam of 31 feet and a depth of 11 feet. The ship was lengthened by 26 feet in 1910.

Superbly fitted, the *America* carried excursion trade between Chicago and Michigan City for her first three years. In 1901, she ran on Lake Erie.

While operating out of Chicago, the *America* caught the eye of Alfred Booth, founder of A. Booth Company of Chicago. He was seeking a newer, faster vessel for the fleet his company sailed along the north

shore of Lake Superior. Booth interests completed the purchase during the winter of 1901.

Greeted by hundreds of town folk when she arrived in Duluth on April 26, 1902, the *America* spent one idle day in port. Then she began her schedule of three weekly runs between Duluth-Superior, Isle Royale and Port Arthur, touching at numerous points along the north shore.

One thing that no ship's carpenter can build into a vessel is promptness — that's the master's responsibility. Captain Jacob Frederick Hector and the *America* made their rounds on time, despite Lake Superior's most treacherous weather and a rugged shoreline route. There were numerous lumps, bumps, near misses and unforeseen circumstances, but the *America* was nearly always on schedule.

When Hector died in 1910, Captain Edward C. "Indian" Smith, formerly the first mate, carried on that reputation. Smith knew his vessel and Lake Superior so well that it was

said he could "smell his way along the north shore." Many noted his ability to navigate in fog, blowing the ship's steam whistle, listening for the echo and knowing exactly when to adjust his course. The *America* would emerge alongside a skiff, hand down the mail and groceries, then disappear. On the return trip she would stop again to pick up fish. An intimate knowledge of the north shore, an excellent pocket watch and a keen ear kept the *America* out of many scrapes which would have claimed a less skilled master and vessel.

The *America* last steamed out of Duluth on June 6, 1928, heading up the north shore, touching at her usual ports of call. From Grand Marais, she headed toward Isle Royale to drop off a number of passengers in the early morning darkness. In all, 10 passengers and 30 crewmen were aboard when she slipped away from the Singer Hotel dock at Washington Island on the southwest end of Isle Royale.

**Right:** *Here is mute evidence of the destructive forces of time, current and ice. The forward 70 feet of the wooden topsides were largely destroyed during the first winter, 1928-29. This added rebuilding costs to the salvage expense, sealing* America's *fate.* **Bottom:** *The companionway, allowing safe passage fore and aft on the main deck level. The missing porthole was a target of early vandalism.* Photos by Bruce Bisping

*At first the pumps appeared to handle the inrushing water, but a reassessment by the chief engineer alerted everyone: the America was going to sink!*

Shortly after clearing the dock, Captain Smith turned the vessel over to First Mate John Wick and retired to his cabin. Five minutes later the ship thudded over a reef, bumping four times and poking a small hole through her single bottom below the engine room. At first the pumps appeared to handle the inrushing water, but a reassessment by the chief engineer alerted everyone: the *America* was going to sink!

Meanwhile, Captain Smith had returned to the bridge where he found an excited and red-faced mate ringing the ship's bell to alert all aboard of the disaster.

"Beach her! Beach her!" Smith yelled, remembering a small gravel beach across Washington Harbor — as good a place as any to nose the ship ashore to prevent foundering in deep water. The wheelsman swung the wheel with all the power he could muster, pointing the *America* directly for the beach, but she ground to a halt about 30 yards short — a misfortune that ultimately

The anchor winches, located on main deck in shallow water. The rectangular assembly at the right is a hatch cover plate and bow vent pipe used in the 1966 salvage attempt. The anchors were removed from the ship in 1942 by the U.S. Army Corps of Engineers for use on a dredge.     Photo by Bruce Bisping

*"Beach her! Beach her!" Smith yelled, remembering a small gravel beach across Washington Harbor — as good a place as any to nose the ship ashore to prevent foundering in deep water.*

prevented her salvage.

The crew moved swiftly, assuring passengers and fellow crewmen that there was no need to panic. Five lifeboats were launched; Captain Smith was the last to leave. From the time of the first damage report at about 3 a.m., it took an hour and a half for the *America* to settle on the rock pinnacle that snagged her for a second time. The only casualty was a water spaniel which was tied in the aft and drowned as the stern settled below the surface.

Investigations by the ship's owners and the U.S. Steamboat Inspection Service followed. Ultimately, it was determined that First Mate Wick chose a course too close to shore in the early morning darkness, and he was censured for careless navigation. No other officers shared fault.

The Ft. William *Daily Times Journal* carried the most fitting epitaph for the *America,* saying "...It was the *America* which did the local, routine work along the north shore, poking her nose into every little har-

bor on the coast line and keeping communication between the mainland and Isle Royale uninterrupted. ...She was like the local train which unloads its freight at every unimportant siding, past which the stately express glides as if it never existed."

Booth Fisheries announced on June 12 that insurance firms were seeking bids for the ship. Whether any salvage firms really got excited about the *America* is not clear, but Captain Cornelius O. Flynn, vessel master, and his son Paul, a salvage diver, both of Duluth, made the first underwater survey of the ship. He announced plans to raise her and place her back in service on the south shore.

In the interim, underwriters settled with Booth Fisheries for the *America's* hull, but apparently not her cargo. The ship's loss effectively put an end to Booth's Duluth operations.

More than a year after the sinking, Captain Flynn successfully obtained ownership of the *America.* Although

he visited the wreck several times and devised ways to raise her, he was never able to secure the necessary capital for the venture —the Great Depression had descended on the Twin Ports and the nation.

When sunk, the *America* was still protruding above water, technically a stranding rather than a foundering since the wheelhouse and forward deck were left above the surface. Ice damaged this portion over the winters of 1928 and 1929, shearing off the cabins. More important, she was buoyed up by ice in 1929-30, released from the rock and by spring had slipped totally beneath the surface.

Over the ensuing 49 years, the *America* changed little, slipping downward to 85 feet at the stern and four feet at the bow. She now rests at about a 45-degree angle upward and heeled over on the port side.

Flynn's son inherited the *America* and the desire to refloat her, but was unable to fund a salvage attempt. Others, too, considered salvage, and a serious effort was made in 1965

70

**Right:** *Deep inside the* America. *Disturbed silt and marine growth, unavoidable in such close quarters, often confuse and panic divers. Planned dives with a reliable "buddy" reduce such hazards.* **Bottom:** *The curved pipe in front of the diver is a lifeboat davit on the top deck near the* America's *stern. Too deep for ice damage, this portion of the* America *is largely intact.*
Photos by Bruce Bisping

**". . . It was the America which did the local, routine work along the north shore, poking her nose into every little harbor on the coast line and keeping communication between the mainland and Isle Royale uninterrupted."**

with plans to return the ship to the Duluth waterfront as a tourist attraction [see next story]. Actual work was done in the late fall of 1965 but was frustrated by foul weather. When the crew returned, there was a hole in the ship's side, apparently caused by dynamite placed by "an unknown party" to stop salvage of the vessel.

Now, the *America* has thousands of visitors annually. Every summer day, en route from Grand Portage to Isle Royale, Captain Stanley Sivertson halts his passenger boat *Wenonah* over the *America*. There, on a clear day in the shadow of the *Wenonah*, passengers can see down more than 30 feet, easily distinguishing the *America*'s hull, forward hatch opening and her anchor winch.

Hundreds of other visitors become more intimately familiar with the *America* through the increasingly popular sport of diving. Estimates are that more dives are made on the *America* than on all the other wrecks at Isle Royale National Park.  □

# The *America* Salvage Attempt

## *The effort to raise the grand old lady*

by James R. Marshall

**D**ESPITE THE MANY STORIES TO THE CONTRARY, our attempt to salvage the steamer *America* was not a lark, but a sincere endeavor. In the early 1960s I began the research on the sunken steamer I had never seen, only heard about. I learned the wreck, which lies off Isle Royale, Michigan, in Washington Harbor, was still private property, owned by a hard-hat diver named Flynn, who lived in Duluth, Minnesota.

I first met Paul J. Flynn in 1965, when he was in the autumn years of a very full life. Our initial conversation was by telephone. I explained that Chuck McClernan, my son Randy and I had just visited the sunken wreck. I told Paul we were very curious and wanted to meet with him to learn more about the *America*.

"She's ready to come up," Flynn said. "Seal her off, put the air to her and she'll float like a cork."

"Mr. Flynn," I responded, "the *America* has been on the bottom for 27 years. The ice has largely destroyed her forward superstructure; the ship is a mess. Just how do you 'seal her off?'"

We agreed to meet the next day at Paul's home on Skyline Boulevard. Paul's lovely wife, Irene, greeted us at the door, and showed us to seats in the living room.

There followed a series of discussions, over several days, which resulted in my purchase of the sunken vessel "together with the mast, bowsprit, sails, boats and anchors, cables, tackle and all furniture, and all other necessities, thereinto pertaining and belonging, as if and where found in its present condition, as and where it lies on the bottom of Washington Harbor, Isle Royale, Michigan."

Nothing, we soon found, is quite as complicated as assuming — for a fair amount of cash — the ownership of a sunken ship which "a few divers already felt they held title to." When I called my insurance man and described the acquisition, he aged several years.

Flynn didn't stop there. He had "just the boat" for such a salvage attempt — the *Skipper Sam*. My attorney, Pat O'Brien, just shrugged. "You've already mortgaged your hats, spats and wallet. Why not at least have a boat ride!"

The venerable *Skipper Sam*, built in 1940 at Sturgeon Bay, Wisconsin, proved to be a good deal. She was 38 feet of very seaworthy cypress, cedar and white oak, powered by a Graymarine 6-330 gas engine swinging a 20-inch propeller. She made an honest 9.5 statute-miles-an-hour and soon proved far more seaworthy than her very green crew!

From the earliest stages of these discussions, I had kept Minnesota congressman John Blatnik apprised of what we were thinking of doing. He was enthusiastic, and with his help we soon received our National Park Service permit to conduct salvage operations on the *America*. At that time the U.S. Navy was disposing of dozens of World War II submarines, and Congressman Blatnik was certain we should have one to assist in our salvage attempt. An old seaman, Blatnik didn't like the thought of all these subs being scuttled in deep water in the ocean. Sending one to Lake Superior, his backyard, was just the ticket.

My problem was simple: I was having a heck of a time with a 38-foot cruiser. What would we do with 200 feet of surplus submarine? We finally leveled with him — no money, no time, no skills! Much later we learned that he had persuaded the Navy to keep one sub for nearly a year, "just in case."

We gathered a cast of characters even Hollywood would have envied. I had a dive shop which serviced the western end of Lake Superior, and among our customers was a group of Canadian Air Force airmen who were stationed in Duluth. They were quick to accept our invitation to join in this adventure, which was led by Chuck McClernan and Fred Calahan, a Duluth banker whom we swiped for the occasion. Our carpenter was Jim Bronikowski, another Duluthian, who could build a 12-room mansion out of an orange crate. Mike Pinkstaff, a sharp young diver, also joined the group. The Canadians, Pete Robinet, George Slauenwhite, Rick Doyle and Maurice "Moe" Gamblin, thought this might be quite an outing. Helping in the orientation training was Don Franklin, a noted Lake Superior diver who had spent dozens of hours on the sunken *America*.

Not an incidental benefit, we soon found, was the fact that the Canadian government took pity on their "overseas" soldiers by giving them extra leave, overseas pay and their very own liquor store. Forty ounces of excellent Canadian whisky cost, at that store, the lordly sum of $1.35. A six-pack of beer cost $1.65 in those days, and it never failed to amaze the divers visiting Isle Royale that the "crazy Canadians" working on the *America* would trade one for the other. There never was enough beer.

Our plan was reasonably simple. Flynn had been right about sealing up the forward and aft sections. About 60 percent of the hull was not a problem, once the forward main deck area had been cleared of sections of collapsed superstructure. Once she was afloat, we planned to bring her back to Duluth for a complete refurbishing. We would then turn her over to the St. Louis County Historical Society for all to come and see.

By the end of October 1965, we had completed the job of closing her open hatches, forward and aft of the engine area, and were ready to utilize airlifts to pull the water from her bow and stern. A curved plate with a thick gasket had been secured to the original hole which had sunk the boat. Repeated test pumping of both the forward and aft sections aided each time in plugging more small leaks. The whole bow, back to the coal bunkers, was mostly air.

We had given another bundle of our dwindling resources to Yalmer Mattila of Houghton, Michigan, to bring a large air compressor out to the island in his landing craft to provide sufficient air for the project. He was loaded and ready, waiting for

*Charles McClernan (left) and James R. Marshall review newspaper reports in this 1965 photograph taken during the salvage attempt on the* America. *James Marshall Collection.*

our call announcing that the hull had been sealed. We had secured a cable to the bow, tying it to a large boulder ahead of the wreck. This, we felt, would tether the ship until we could move it to the shallows of the adjacent bay. There we would complete the pumping out of the hull and ready the ship for her trip to Duluth. The DM&IR tug *Edna G* had been brought out of mothballs, after a three-year nap in Two Harbors, to help in the tow if needed.

Mattila was ready; we were ready; the lake was not. A "blow" commenced on October 27, 1965, and it blew solid until November 7. The temperature dropped to 5 degrees F, and we reluctantly decided to abandon the salvage attempt until spring.

We had kept the National Park Service and the superintendent fully

informed of our progress, and they were pleased to issue another salvage permit, this time covering the period through July 1, 1966. The *Skipper Sam* arrived back in Duluth on November 16, breaking ice in the boat yard haul-out slip.

During that winter I made numerous slide presentations around Minnesota and Wisconsin, explaining the *America* project. In the Twin Cities, the hostility toward the project was soon apparent. Some old diving friends cautioned me, saying that the hate developing toward us and the desire to keep the *America* just where she lay was becoming a fervent cause.

Finally the problem surfaced in a heated exchange in the WCCO radio studios in Minneapolis. It seems that the way the *America* lay, with her

# . . . I sometimes sense the very real presence of Paul Flynn, dressed in his battered diving dress.

bow a scant two feet under water, was quite an attraction to many would-be divers in the Twin Cities. They could get all togged up in their wet suits, swim the 100 feet from shore to the bow and be photographed clutching the buoy in a most daring pose. We were taking away their toy!

One diver, boasting of having all the tools from the engine room of the *America* in his basement, swore with clenched fist he would "throw them in the Mississippi" rather than return them, if we floated the ship.

In early April 1966, a friend from Grand Portage reported that a mystery truck and boat had been seen. The boat had been launched in the dark and was back before noon, when it was loaded up and hauled away.

The *Skipper Sam,* sporting a radio, depth finder and new galley, arrived at the Grace Island Base Camp in Washington Harbor on May 3, 1966. A new heavy-duty scuba tank air compressor was put to work, and Chuck McClernan went out to the *America* to place mooring buoys on the wreck.

As was our custom, each diver was paired with a diving buddy, one to watch and one to work. We would always dive in pairs to the exposed propeller, which was at a depth of 85 feet. This was mainly a psychological exercise because the boat lay at an angle on an underground hill and the depth almost anywhere a diver went within the hull would never be as deep as at the propeller.

Chuck made the first dive, searching for our old enemy, monofilament fishing line, which is invisible under water and was often snagged on the wreck.

His buddy was barely in the water

when Chuck surfaced. "Something is very wrong," he said. "The propeller is almost completely buried." We looked at each other. In 1965, the propeller was just slightly covered with gravel; two of the blades carried the scratched names of numerous divers.

Further inspection disclosed that the propeller shaft tube was also distorted and the hull was folded on one side. It became obvious that the *America* had tried to slide further down into the trench between the main island and Thompson Island. But what had caused this? Ice? We swam toward the bow. The problem was soon obvious.

After a winter's cover of ice, Lake Superior's bottom is heavily laden with sediment. Before us in a great arc from the area about a third of the way aft, the bottom was as clean as a wave-washed beach. Further inspection disclosed that an explosive charge had been placed between the supports for the deck winches and the skin of the boat, tearing a Y-shaped hole in the hull, just above the keel.

We reported this to the National Park Service, which soon had visions of the next world war being fought at Isle Royale. That day we began the arduous task of digging a trench to the new wound, which became a 77-foot-long ditch over three feet deep. We gathered a batch of old mattresses and finally sealed the hull.

The Park Service had a bombing party, and invited some real hightest friends. The FBI and a pair of U.S. Navy divers arrived in late June,

telling us they had heard of numerous threats of a "booby trap," an additional bomb in the hull.

After two months of repairing and waiting, our funds were running out. It was pump the *America* soon or else.

"Or else" arrived in the form of a letter from the U.S. District Attorney, Grand Rapids, Michigan. In essence, it decried the act of bombing at Isle Royale and challenged our ownership of the now controversial vessel. Furthermore, it said, no additional permits would be issued pending resolution of the issues raised in the letter.

It was over. We were essentially broke, our attorney had been named to the bench, the Canadians were out of leave time and a persistent ear infection affected almost all of the divers. It was a sad and quiet trip home in the *Skipper Sam.*

It is too late now, in the late 1980s, for the *America.* Generations of divers have stolen everything removable from her ice-battered hull, and she has rolled another 10 degrees onto her side. She has claimed one diver so far, trapped in the dumbwaiter between the galley and the dining room. The superstructure above the engine is a rotting time bomb, which we hope will collapse under the weight of ice and not on some unsuspecting diver. In my annual visits, I sometimes sense the very real presence of Paul Flynn, dressed in his battered diving dress.

"Seal her up, Jim, and pump her out," he says with a grin. "She'll float like a cork!"

□

# Duluth's Doorstep Shipwreck

**The Thomas Wilson "sails the bottom" of Lake Superior less than a mile from the ship canal**

by Paul von Goertz
**historical photos from the Ken Thro collection**

**I** CAN REMEMBER, AS A BOY growing up next to Lake Superior in Duluth, hearing stories about boats that were sunk within view of the city. Nobody seemed to have any particulars about the wrecks, other than that they were just "there." Somebody said one of the wrecks was a boat that had sunk with a load of cars and that if it were ever found, someone would have an instant antique car collection —

although probably limited to just one car model.

Well, for whatever you might have heard about shipwrecks at the western tip of Lake Superior, there is only one openwater wreck — the whaleback steamer *Thomas Wilson*. There were other wrecks, maybe three or four vessels that were beached and battered by merciless nor'easters between Duluth and Two Harbors, but all were refloated

**Above:** *The* Wilson *anchor recovery team examines its prize on board the Coast Guard Cutter* Woodrush *minutes after the successful salvage in 1973. Left to right: David Anderson of Superior; the author, Paul von Goertz, Knife River; Elmer Engman, Dive Master from Duluth; and Dan Goman, also from Duluth.*
**Inset:** *The* Wilson *on her launch date on April 30, 1892, in Superior, Wisconsin. She was named after Captain Thomas Wilson, an old friend of the ship's builder, Captain Alexander McDougall.*

and/or salvaged in part or in whole.

Now, shipwreck purists will remind me that there is another vessel sunk between Duluth and Two Harbors, and that this is the "ghost ship" *Benjamin Noble,* claimed with all hands by a nor'easter in 1914. This is true, but her exact location has never been established, and she probably will never be found.

In this century, Duluth has had at least three noteworthy doorstep incidents involving bulk freighters, the most recent being the *M/V Socrates* beached in Duluth in 1985 which, thankfully, ended without loss of life or property. The most spectacular doorstep shipwreck was the steamer *Mataafa* blown perpendicular across the Duluth piers, beached and broken in half by a vicious nor'easter in November of 1905. Nine men froze to death on her before a rescue attempt could be made, even though Duluthians burned high bonfires in what is now Canal Park to rally the spirits of the brave crew.

The third doorstep shipwreck was the wreck of the *Thomas Wilson.* And I'm sure it would have been as spectacular as the wreck of the *Mataafa,* had one seen it. But you would have had to be looking at just the right instant, because the whole disaster was over in less than three minutes. The horror of the whole incident is particularly poignant when you consider that the 308-foot vessel and nine of her crew were on the bottom of the lake even before the vessel's bow wave reached shore from the collision site.

The *Wilson* became a permanent guest of the big lake as a result of one of the most freakish and tragic marine disasters ever on Lake Superior. At 10:40 a.m. on Saturday, June 7, 1902, a day when the lake was unusually calm and the sky was clear, the *Wilson* was involved in a collision with the wooden steamer *George Hadley.* The circumstances of the collision seem incredible.

A few moments before the *Wilson* was to clear the entry downbound from Duluth, deeply laden with

*In 1973, the author, as a member of the artifacts committee for the then new Duluth Marine Museum, worked with three other local divers to recover an anchor off the* **Wilson** *for presentation to the museum. The anchor was originally spotted lying on the bottom, free of the wreck, by diver Elmer Engman of Duluth. A total of 15 separate dives were necessary to prepare the anchor for lifting off the bottom.*

*Through the influence of the late Ralph Knowlton of Duluth, a retired official with the U.S. Corps of Engineers and a founder of the Duluth Marine Museum, the United States Coast Guard Cutter* Woodrush *was made available to lift the one-and-one-half-ton anchor free from the lake bottom. The anchor is displayed today in Canal Park.*

*A note of caution:*

*I cannot let anyone reading about my diving expriences on the* Wilson *believe such diving can be attempted by an inexperienced diver. It is a very dangerous dive because of very poor visibility, currents, danger of entanglement in debris and passing vessel traffic. On my last dive on the* Wilson *in 1974, I became lost in the cold darkness while inside the vessel. I fought the urge to panic three, four, five times and finally fought my way out. I surfaced in the bright warm sunshine with my wetsuit covered with rust, and with less than 30 pounds of air pressure in an air tank which when full contained more than 2,000 pounds. I made one more wreck dive after this incident, but the fear I had experienced with the last* Wilson *dive still haunted me. A month later I sold all of my scuba gear. I have not dived since.*

more than 3,000 tons of rich natural iron ore, the tugboat *Annie L. Smith* was dispatched to meet the upbound steamer *George Hadley* with instructions for the *Hadley* to not enter the harbor by the Duluth entry, but rather to make a 90-degree left turn and head for the Superior entry.

What Captain Fitzgerald of the *Hadley* did upon receiving his instruction is hard to comprehend. Both vessels were approaching one another for what should have been a normal passing situation. Captain Fitzgerald, perhaps from a sitting position on the bridge of the *Hadley*

where he couldn't see the deep-laden *Wilson,* ordered his wheelsman to make a sharp port turn and make for the Superior entry. With this order he turned the *Hadley* directly into the path of the *Wilson.*

Captain Cameron of the *Wilson,* probably blinking with disbelief, ordered an evasive sharp starboard turn. The two vessels cut identical semicircular arcs; where the arcs intersected, the vessels collided.

The wooden prow of the *Hadley* caught the *Wilson* in the center on her port side with such force that she rode partly over the *Wilson,* inflicting a mortal wound. With her tons of momentum, the *Wilson* continued forward, clumsily dragging the *Hadley* impaled on her side.

As the *Wilson* began to fill, she slowed, and when the bow of the *Hadley* broke free of the *Wilson,* "with a tremendous jerk," the *Wilson* sank like the rock she was carrying.

The journalists writing in the Duluth newspaper at the time relate: "As she plunged, the crew that was still aboard her continued to undress and rushed to the stern jumping overboard as fast as they could free themselves from their clothing."

Captain Cameron was nearly pulled under by the suction of the stricken vessel, but when the boilers exploded, he was blown clear. With propeller "still spinning at a terrific rate," the *Wilson* "rolled" and headed bow first to the bottom. At least one man was seen drawn into the spinning propeller.

In less than three minutes the *Wilson* was gone. The *Hadley* maintained engine power and buoyancy long enough to pick up survivors and beach herself in 24 feet of water one block south of the Duluth entry.

Of the 20 men that comprised the *Wilson's* crew, nine were lost. Only two of the nine bodies were recovered. The remaining seven are entombed to this day in the hull of the *Wilson.*

The *Wilson* rests quietly on the bottom of Lake Superior in 70 feet of water, $7/8$ mile from the end of the

**Above:** *The aft mast of the* Wilson *rises hauntingly from the bottom of Lake Superior in this photo taken a few days after she was sunk by the wooden steamer* George Hadley *on June 7, 1902, off the Duluth harbor entry.* **Right:** *The* Wilson *passing through the locks at Sault Ste. Marie, Michigan.*

canal piers, nearly diagonal to the shipping lanes with her bow pointing north and her stern south. I can say the *Wilson* "rests quietly" on the bottom of the lake because that is how she appeared to me when I first saw her as a scuba diver in 1970. I was an active scuba diver at that time, completely enamored of the wreck of the *Wilson* and other Lake Superior wrecks. To be on the *Wilson* was a thrill, because she remains in pretty good shape, although a good part of her wooden superstructure was removed by dynamite as a navigational hazard. When she sank, the top of her smokestack was only ten feet underwater.

The bow turret, the three aft turrets upon which the wooden structure sat and the 308-foot-long hull remain nearly intact.

For the experienced diver with the right equipment, entry into the forward bow turret and the two aftermost turrets is possible. To the best of my knowledge, entry has not been gained into the turret housing the boiler room. A safe guess would be that the men entombed in the wreck might be found in the boiler room, as this was the compartment nearest the actual point of collision.

The preservation qualities of ice cold Lake Superior have protected the old wreck well. (Lake Superior's

cold water jokingly has been referred to as existing in either of two states — frozen ice or melted ice. But to a diver it's not funny — it's cold.)

On one dive, I examined some wooden planking near the stern. The wood was not in the least rotted and even the putty in the seams was intact. I was amazed.

**B**lack and white paint is easily distinguishable and the brass in her engine room and around her portholes appears only slightly affected after more than 85 years on the bottom. Her steel hull and turrets are rusted and pitted but not as much as one might expect. One could safely speculate that the cold water would also preserve the remains of the seven sailors entombed in her belly.

The *Wilson* sits on an even keel and appears to be down by the stern either because of the illusion created by the silt piled around her stern or because her stern has perhaps sunk into the silt.

She's defied two salvage attempts, one in the late 1930s, one in 1962. Chances are she'll be there until she rusts through, as anyone interested in salvaging her for her ore will find that today's blast furnace needs are different from those of 1902.

The next time you view the big lake off the Duluth piers, let your imagination drift a little. Maybe you can visualize the whaleback quietly "sailing the bottom" while modern lake vessels three times her size cut a path directly above her.

If you have a boat with a depth sounder, you can easily find the wreck. Here's the triangulation: draw a line from Enger Tower and the light on the north pier of the Duluth entry, then bisect that line with a line that forms when you can see through both windows of the west turret of the pavilion in Leif Erickson Park.

I usually found the *Wilson* by following the line from Enger Tower and the north pier out into the lake until I reached 70 feet of water. Then suddenly the sounder would jump from 70 feet to 55 feet. That 55-foot reading is the deck of the *Wilson.* You can follow the 55-foot reading in a north and south direction for the full 308-foot length of the vessel.

It is an eerie feeling to be above the wreck, knowing that 55 feet below in the cold dark waters of Lake Superior lies a good ship and nearly half of her crew, victims of a disaster that laid the *Wilson* at Duluth's doorstep, and a place in the maritime heritage of the City of Duluth.  □

# Museums and
# Preserves

*The Marine Museum is Minnesota's most popular attraction.* Photo courtesy Canal Park Marine Museum

# Preserving the Wrecks Through Museums

**M**USEUMS. **THEY PROVIDE A PUBLIC CONTACT** with items that generally are remote and unobtainable. In the case of shipwrecks, the artifacts and ship remains are only accessible to technically qualified divers. Museums are often our only contact with this nether world of the past.

*A section of the diving exhibit at the Canal Park Museum.* Photo courtesy Canal Park Marine Museum

## Canal Park Marine Museum Duluth, Minnesota

Duluth's Canal Park Museum is a free service of the U.S. Army Corps of Engineers' Detroit District, administered under the nationwide Corps Visitors Center Program. It is open year round, although the schedules vary with the season. The museum attracts some of the largest crowds in Minnesota.

The museum was built in 1973 and enlarged in 1979, with 15,000 square feet of exhibit space and more than 10,000 artifacts. Among the attractions are a two-story steam engine salvaged from a retired tugboat, a full-sized ship's pilothouse, three historic ship-cabin replicas, hundreds of shipwreck artifacts and more than 40 fine, to-scale ship models. Much of the support for the popular waterfront facility has been coordinated by the Lake Superior Marine Museum Association, an auxiliary with membership of more than 600.

The museum provides a number of educational services, including vessel commentary, 24-hour Boat-watchers' Hotline (218-722-6489), films, lectures and group tours. Inquiries can be made at 218-727-2497. Reservations are required for group services.

## Great Lakes Shipwreck Museum Whitefish Point, Michigan

The Great Lakes Shipwreck Historical Society was formed in 1978 to produce programs to educate the public about Great Lakes' shipwrecks, their preservation and interpretation of maritime history. The society operates a museum located at the Whitefish Point Lighthouse where the focus is on ships that sank nearby.

The Whitefish Point Lighthouse was the earliest on Lake Superior. It entered service in 1849, six years before the opening of the first shipping lock at Sault Ste. Marie. In 1973, it was placed on the National Register of Historic Places.

Thomas L. Farnquist is president of the society, with headquarters in Sault Ste. Marie, Michigan. An active diver, his primary interest is documenting on film the diveable wrecks around Whitefish Point. Through donations from private foundations, corporations and the public, the museum continues to present artifacts and the historical footage obtained by the society.

The museum is open from late May until October 15. Additional information is available by writing to the Great Lakes Shipwreck Historical Society, Route 2, Box 279-A, Sault Ste. Marie, Michigan 49783.

*Underwater photographer Terry Begnoche (right) assists Thomas Farnquist (left) in preparation for a dive on a Whitefish Bay wreck. In the background, diver Gary Shumbarger prepares the camera equipment.* Photo courtesy Great Lakes Shipwreck Historical Society

*One of the displays at the Whitefish Point Museum.* Photo courtesy of Great Lakes Shipwreck Historical Society

**Below:** *In the early 1900s, the whaleback was the prime mover of iron ore on the Great Lakes.* Courtesy Canal Park Marine Museum
**Right:** *The SS* Meteor, *the last remaining whaleback, was converted to a museum in 1973.* Courtesy Head of the Lakes Maritime Society

## S.S. Meteor Marine Museum Superior, Wisconsin

It's possible to step back in time to the age of the "pigboat," or whaleback, a flat-bottomed ship with rounded sides and snout-like bow. In fact, it's possible to step inside a whaleback to see what life was like on the lakes at the turn of the century.

The Head of the Lakes Maritime Society maintains the *Meteor*. This is the last remaining whaleback, converted in 1973 to a museum on Superior's waterfront at Barker's Island. Guided tours of the ship reveal the secrets of Captain Alexander McDougall's design. He envisioned a ship of steel, faster than the conventional wooden vessels then in use, that would move through the water with less friction and offer minimal resistance to waves and weather.

Today thousands of visitors can climb through this relic of the past. Daily tours are available during the summer and early fall. For more information, contact the S.S. *Meteor* Museum on Barker's Island at 715-392-5642. □

**M**OST **M**HISTORICAL **artifacts speak to us silently from shelves and behind glass in the shelter of museums.** But those under water have, until recently, been subject not only to the transforming power of wave action and temperature change, but also to the passion of souvenir and treasure hunters.

Now a magnificent collection of Lake Superior shipwrecks is safe from vandalism and salvage within an edifice of law. Called the Alger Underwater Preserve, the underwater museum's holdings range from near-intact wooden ore carriers to graceful wooden schooners.

The preserve came into being in 1980 when the Michigan legislature passed and Governor William Milliken signed the Underwater Preserve Act. This law directed the state to "...protect and preserve, and to regulate the taking of aboriginal records and antiquities within this state; to preserve abandoned property of historical or recreational

# Alger Underwater Preserve

## *Lake Superior's paradise for divers*

**written and photographed by Frederick Stonehouse**

value on the bottomlands of the Great Lakes and regulate the salvage of abandoned property of historical or recreational value; and to prescribe penalties."

The Underwater Salvage Committee of the Michigan Department of Natural Resources (DNR) recommended to the state's Natural

Resources Commission that several areas be designated as Great Lakes bottomlands preserves. The most important area accepted was that in Alger County near the small town of Munising, one of the most popular diving locations in the Great Lakes. Its jawbreaker official name, the Alger Great Lakes Bottomland Preserve, has been popularly altered to the Alger Underwater Preserve.

The vital groundwork for selection of the Alger area was achieved by a volunteer citizens' committee with representatives of local divers, dive charter and shop owners, the Alger County Chamber of Commerce, Pictured Rocks National Lakeshore, Michigan State University Extension Service and county historians. This ad hoc citizens group evaluated the area closely. They considered the variety and amount of material and/or cultural features, historical and recreational significance, diving quality, public support, economic impact, management

---

**Top:** *A diver explores the schooner* Granada, *also known as the* Dreadnaught. *The wreck is located in Murray Bay at Grand Island in the Alger Underwater Preserve.*

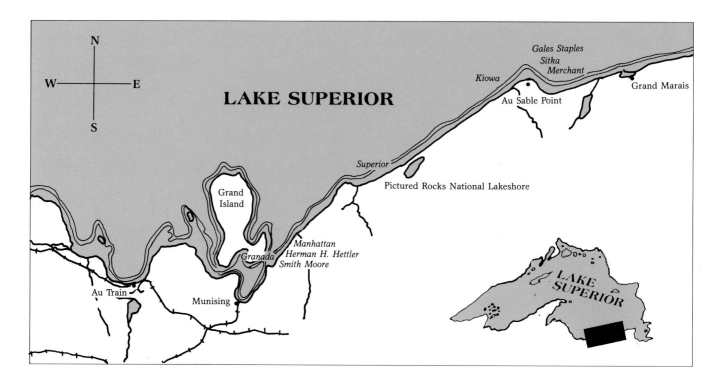

## LAKE SUPERIOR

N
W — E
S

Kiowa
Gales Staples
Sitka
Merchant
Grand Marais
Au Sable Point

Superior
Pictured Rocks National Lakeshore

Grand Island

Manhattan
Herman H. Hettler
Smith Moore

Granada

Au Train

Munising

LAKE SUPERIOR

### ALGER UNDERWATER PRESERVE

potential, threatened resources, proximity to major population areas, complementary onshore recreational facilities and the knowledge about underwater resources. These same criteria were later used by the Natural Resources Commission.

The citizens' committee still functions as a vital conduit of local management initiatives to the state. It has established a wreck buoy system, conducted diver interest surveys, publicized the preserve, searched for new underwater shipwreck and geological assets and organized and rehearsed a diver emergency evacuation plan.

The area of the preserve runs roughly from Au Train Point east to Au Sable Point, to include Munising Bay and the offshore waters of Grand Island. It has a total of 113 square miles of crystal clear diving. Contained within it are some of the most historic and recreationally valuable shipwrecks in the Great Lakes.

The area offers numerous attractions for non-divers, the foremost being the world famous Pictured Rocks National Lakeshore. Half a million people visit the Lakeshore annually. Some hike

*Of an estimated three million sport divers in the United States, one-quarter live in the Great Lakes area. The Alger Underwater Preserve is within a day's drive for all of them.*

the rugged trails and climb the shifting sand dunes, while others marvel at the truly spectacular 200-foot-high rock cliffs from the comfort of fast tour boats.

Other attractions include lighthouses, waterfalls and historic fur trading cabins.

Deep fishing for "lunker" lake trout is near legendary in the local waters.

Critical to the success of the preserve from a diver's point of view are five fully licensed dive charter boat operators, a complete service dive shop, boat livery and public launch site and nearby motels and restaurants.

Of an estimated three million sport divers in the United States, one-quarter live in the Great Lakes area. The Alger Underwater Preserve is within a day's drive for all of them. In 1985 about 6,000 dove the preserve waters to explore its treasures.

The most popular wreck is that of the 223-foot wooden ore carrier *Smith Moore.* The big steamer was lost in Munising's East Channel as the result of a fog collision with the steamer *James Pickands* on July 13, 1889. Resting in 110 feet of water, the wreck is nearly intact and a prime example of a style of vessel that has long

---

**Top Right:** *Exploring an unknown schooner covered by sand near Grand Island.* **Bottom right:** *Although heavily damaged by ice, the wreck of the* Granada *is nearly intact. It is a popular training wreck for novice divers.*

Soon after he left his ship, the lifeboat capsized in the breaking seas, throwing the captain and three crewmen into the freezing water where they disappeared from sight. Reportedly the captain's body was found the following spring, frozen into a block of ice.

since passed from the Great Lakes scene. Her 85-foot deck and hull are still in place except for the shattered port quarter of the bow, the result of the terrible impact with the *Pickands*.

The collision between the two vessels was typical of many such disasters that occurred on the Great Lakes before the days of radar. The *Smith Moore*, running at full speed in fog, was 10 miles north of Grand Island and downbound on the lakes with a heavy cargo of iron ore from Marquette when the *Pickands* materialized out of the fog and plowed into her. Although filling quickly with water, the *Moore* struggled south for safety at Grand Island, only to fall several hundred yards short of grounding snugly on the nearby Sand Point Bar. Shuddering as if in final regret, the steamer dove for the bottom of the channel, allowing barely enough time for her crew to hastily abandon her.

Water visibility for diving on the *Smith Moore* is usually excellent, frequently ranging to 40 feet or more. This clarity is typical of all of the preserve's wrecks.

*If the legend is true, there is a good chance that the historic* Merchant *is somewhere in the preserve, a hidden treasure waiting to be discovered.*

To the northeast of the *Smith Moore* and inshore of Grand Island are the wrecks of the wooden steamers *Manhattan*, lost on October 23, 1903, and *Herman H. Hettler*, coming to grief in nearly the same location 25 years later.

The *Manhattan* was running outside of the channel after sheltering from a storm, when her steering chains broke,

causing her to veer suddenly off course and plow directly onto a rock reef. An oil lamp was overturned by the force of the grounding and started a roaring fire which consumed the vessel.

The *Hettler* was also outbound in the channel when her compass reportedly "deviated," throwing her off course. Whether it was a true deviation or an error in reading the compass by the wheelsman is open to question. But for the steamer *Hettler* the results were the same. Stuck fast to the reef, she was quickly destroyed by fall storms.

Divers can explore the wrecks of both vessels, scattered over 10 acres of the bottom. Included in the debris are hull sections, rudders, planks, framing, ribs and machinery. It's a shipwreck junk yard.

Murray Bay at Grand Island holds another of the preserve's famous wrecks. Locally known as the schooner *Dreadnaught*, it

**Top:** *The freighter* Kiowa *was tipped on her beam ends during a violent northwester on November 30, 1929. She sank after hitting a reef off Au Sable Point. [painting by Ed Pusick]* **Top right:** *A diver explores part of the* Kiowa's *cargo hold, which contained a load of flax.* **Bottom right:** *The sidewheeler* Superior *was lost in October 1856 near Spray Falls. Her boilers and a few other artifacts remain to amaze divers.*

**86**

Contained within it are some of the most historic and recreationally valuable shipwrecks in the Great Lakes.

The wreck of the *Superior* is significant, because it is one of the very few surviving examples of a Great Lakes sidewheeler.

**ALGER UNDERWATER PRESERVE**

was recently reidentified as the *Granada*. Although the name of the wreck may not have been certain, that of Murray Bay is well established. It was named for Father John Murray, a defrocked priest with a reported unquenchable thirst for communion wine. Exiled to the wild and desolate north woods in 1845, he spent his final days teaching school for the children of early settlers.

Like the *Smith Moore*, the *Granada* is also nearly intact, although the masts and deck houses are long gone, and the deck has been heavily ice damaged. Since the wreck is in a mere 15 feet of water, a level at which ice damage is common, the destruction is understandable. The *Granada* is still a photographer's dream and a fine training wreck for novice divers to practice penetrations.

In the shallows just off Spray Falls, one of the many spectacular waterfalls of the Pictured Rocks National

Lakeshore, are the battered remains of the old sidewheeler *Superior*. Upbound from the Soo, she was disabled in a fierce October 1856 storm. Helpless, the *Superior* was forced by wind and wave into the sharp rock cliffs near the waterfall, where she was ground to pieces. By the time the storm slackened the next day, an estimated 36 of her passengers and crew had drowned. The exact death toll is unknown.

The wreck of the *Superior* is significant, because it is one of the very few surviving examples of a Great Lakes sidewheeler. Most of the wreckage is in shallow water, in depths of five to 30 feet. Some pieces can be found directly under the waterfall, making the dive a singular experience. Still visible are the ribs, hull timbers, numerous

**The *Granada* is still a photographer's dream and a fine training wreck for novice divers to practice penetrations.**

iron fittings and small artifacts such as buttons, screws and coins, as well as two large tubed boilers. But often the wreckage is covered by the shifting sands of Superior's bottom, leaving no evidence of this terrible disaster of another century.

Near the eastern boundary of the preserve, just west of Au Sable Point, is the wreckage of the 251-foot steel freighter *Kiowa*. On November 30, 1929,

the *Kiowa* was downbound from Duluth for Chicago with a full cargo of flax, when a roaring northwester caused the cargo to shift, rolling the steamer on her beam-ends. With imminent foundering seeming the only outcome, the captain with several crewmen attempted to go for help in the only lifeboat. It proved to be a tragic decision.

Soon after he left his ship, the lifeboat capsized in the breaking seas, throwing the captain and three crewmen into the freezing water where they disappeared from sight. Reportedly the captain's body was found the following spring, frozen into a block of ice. But fate smiled on the remaining stranded crew. The sinking *Kiowa* drifted faster than they realized and soon fetched up on a reef off lonely Au Sable Point. The next day, in calmer seas, the crew was rescued by the Grand Marais Coast Guard.

Shattered by storms, the *Kiowa* spilled her rich grain cargo into the lake. Instead of becoming a pollutant, the flax was greedily eaten by the local lake trout and whitefish, forming a major part of their winter diet. In the spring, when local commercial fishermen again set nets and hauled in heavy catches, they discovered that the fish had a decided flavor of linseed oil, evidently the result of their unusual diet. However, since the fishermen marketed their catch far to the south in major cities like Chicago, no special attention was paid to the phenomenon. After all, they weren't eating the fish!

The *Kiowa* wreck is an excellent example of the awesome power of storm and ice on Lake Superior. What was once a proud creation of man,

**Top:** *The Au Sable lighthouse stands a lonely vigil to protect ships from the damaging reefs of the Point.*

built of the best steel to withstand half a century of hard use on the Great Lakes and high seas, has been reduced to metallic rubble. The massive bow winch and anchor chain, as well as shaft and pillow block, are still present. The propeller and engine were salvaged after the wreck.

Also in Au Sable Point waters are the remains of several wooden wrecks. Au Sable was infamous for treacherous, pea soup fogs, a natural result of the warmer air spilling down from 200-foot-high sand dunes and mixing with the much colder air over the lake. When a thick blanket of fog covered the sandy outreach of the point, a deadly hazard was formed. Unable to determine their true courses, many ships slammed into the point's outer reefs to eventually become wrecks. Notable among them are the wooden freighters *Sitka*, sliding up on Au Sable in October 1904 with an iron ore cargo, and the coal-carrying steamer *Gales Staples* in 1918. Both vessels were total losses and today provide popular diving targets.

Some historians feel there is a possibility that somewhere within the preserve boundaries is the long-missing schooner *Merchant*. Lost in June 1847, the *Merchant* is perhaps the most historic shipwreck on Superior, an early example of the Great Lakes shipbuilders' art. Upbound with a cargo of heavy mining machinery consigned to the rich copper mines of the Keweenaw Peninsula, she and her 14-man crew literally sailed into history as the first vessel on Lake Superior to just disappear, or in popular period terms, "go missing." A broken piece of her companionway was found floating near the north shore four months later. It was all

that was ever located from her. A persistent Indian legend tells of a small vessel foundering near Grand Island in a sudden squall. If the legend is true, there is a good chance that the historic *Merchant* is somewhere in the preserve, a hidden treasure waiting to be discovered.

The preserve has a total of 21 known wrecks and perhaps yet another five undiscovered ones. This certainly ranks it high as a rich collection of maritime history.

The only major type of vessel missing from the preserve's underwater collection is a steel ore carrier. The preserve committee is actively working towards adding one. Properly detoxified of pollutants and altered to minimize hazards, such a vessel would be an underwater cultural interpretative asset. Placed on an even keel so that the pilothouse would be at the 40-foot depth and the spar deck at 80 feet, it would be easily and safely accessible to divers.

Just think of it! In a single day, a diver could examine the entire history of Lake Superior transportation from early schooners to sidewheeler, wooden ore carriers to a steel freighter, all within the confines of the Alger Underwater Preserve.  □

# Alger Underwater Preserve

## Dive Charter Operators:

**Grand Island Ventures**
Peter J. Lindquist
RR1, Box 436
Mill Street
Munising, Michigan 49862
906-387-4477

**Tomasi Tours**
George Tomasi
455 E. Ridge Street
Marquette, Michigan 49855
906-225-0410

**Aqua Cats**
Rick Steinhauer
408 Sunset Drive
DeForest, Wisconsin 53532
608-846-4691

**3 Little Devils**
Fred Marty
1011 20th Avenue
Monroe, Wisconsin 53566
608-325-6477

## Boat Livery:

**Oscar Froberg**
P.O. Box 86
Munising, Michigan 49862
906-387-4587

## Dive Shop/Boat Livery:

**Sea & Ski Scuba**
Bob & Judy Cromell
P.O. Box 64
Munising, Michigan 49862
906-387-2927

## Public Tours:

**Pictured Rocks Boat Cruises**
Munising, Michigan 49862
Three cruise boats
June through October, weather permitting
906-387-2379

*This diver seems insignificant next to the boilers of the* Cumberland, *which sank in Isle Royale's Washington Harbor on July 23, 1877.* Photo courtesy of Submerged Cultural Resources Unit

# Isle Royale's Submerged History

## *An experience in preservation*
### by Kenneth J. Vrana

VIEWED FROM A FLOAT PLANE, MICHIGAN'S ISLE ROYALE resembles a flotilla of small islands and reefs, guarding a massive upheaval of volcanic rock. Over 40 miles long and up to 10 miles wide, it dominates northwestern Lake Superior.

From its rock fissures, natives of old hammered out malleable red metal used for weapons or items of adornment. Later, Europeans sought copper for progress, lumber to build great midwestern cities and plentiful fisheries to feed migrating masses.

All of these endeavors touched Isle Royale, although for only a fleeting moment. The spirit of industry was eventually worn thin by realities of a remote, severe environment. However, the primitive beauty of nature was undeniable. Brave travelers ventured to these islands by sail and steamer to revel in feelings of tranquility and timelessness. These sentiments were so powerful that Congress reserved Isle Royale National Park for public enjoyment in perpetuity. Further protection came when "wilderness" status was granted to the northwoods archipelago.

But there's another face to Isle Royale that is sculptured by human ideals and effort and intimately intertwined with every era of its history. The boat. From Indian canoe to fishing skiff and large bulk carriers, life of that region has revolved around its usage.

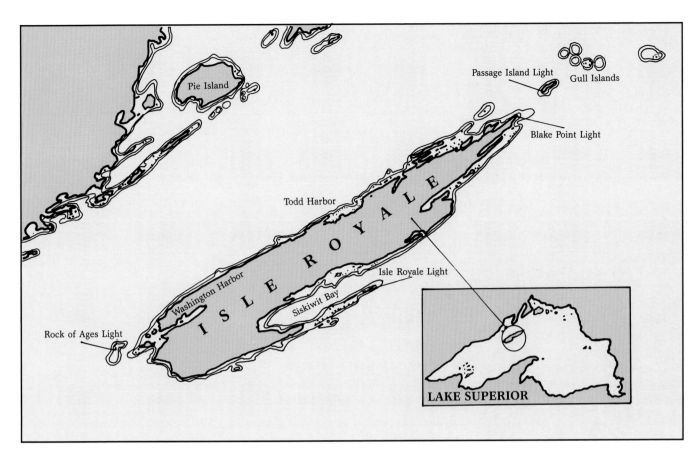

Captains unable to master their boat's own peculiar personality in harmony with Lake Superior's moods often failed, some fatally. Heavy fogs and unforgiving seas served as accomplices to waiting sharp rock reefs. Experienced sailors barely had time for prayer when lake waters claimed another victim.

These incidents, many associated with tragedy, have provided an underwater heritage of unique and intriguing dimensions. Cold, fresh Lake Superior water preserves shipwrecks in a condition unequaled by salt water casualties. Vessels display evidence of wood craftsmanship and metal technology applied decades ago. Other submerged sites associated with prehistoric inhabitants, fur trading, commercial fishing or the resort era await the discriminating view of archaeologists.

The importance of these submerged cultural resources has only recently been fully recognized. Park management of the late 1950s and early '60s was either uninterested or unaware of their importance for recreational sport diving and archaeological research. Personnel concentrated on providing visitor accommodations and services for the infant national park. A series of proposed commercial salvage operations on Isle Royale shipwrecks and

*Cold, fresh Lake Superior water preserves shipwrecks in a condition unequaled by salt water casualties. Vessels display evidence of wood craftmanship and metal technology applied decades ago.*

outcries from a concerned diving public finally forced serious attention by park administrators.

The most controversial affair involved an attempt by Duluth businessmen, aided by political figures, to raise the freight and passenger steamer *America*. She was a beloved friend among fishermen and residents of Minnesota's North Shore, including Isle Royale. The sleek steel vessel could squeeze into harbors too small for larger craft, delivering indispensable groceries and hardware while picking up boxes of whitefish or lake trout. While en route to Thunder Bay, Ontario, *America* nudged a reef in Isle Royale's Washington Harbor. Captain Edward C. Smith ordered the vessel grounded, where it slowly sank. Salvage plans called for return of *America* to Duluth as a floating museum and restaurant. Resistance to this idea came from a growing number of divers, who wished the vessel to remain underwater for sport exploration.

Efforts to raise *America* sparked National Park Service administrators to debate jurisdiction over Isle Royale shipwrecks and the recreational implications of diving. In 1967, continued salvage operations were cancelled by park officials, who claimed full managerial control over submerged cultural resources. This confusing application of authority over

Isle Royale shipwrecks, plus a prevalent ethic of "treasure hunting" among sport divers, resulted in removal of many artifacts and irreplaceable historical information. The *Milwaukee Journal* account of a 1964 dive on the bulk freighter *Emperor,* entitled "Sunken Treasure Hunt" is an example:

"We all swam down to where the pilot house used to be....

"Art went in and returned with a running light and a taffrail log....When we reached Ed and Art at the safe we found them trying to dislodge it from the surrounding debris. They had the line secured and when the safe was finally freed we guided it to the surface. . . . By hammering and chiseling we finally broke the door off. Inside we found the ship's keys and eight $10 Canadian bills, wet but in good shape. We were disappointed, feeling that there should have been more." [*Milwaukee Journal,* January 10, 1965.]

Frequent voices of diving "preservationists" were becoming louder and more demanding. "Our club wishes to see the shipwrecks of Isle Royale preserved for future divers to explore and wonder at. The thrill and adventure of seeing a wreck in its 'natural' state is a thrill that no diver will soon forget. . . . A picture is worth a thousand words, a souvenir good only to a select few. And a camera leaves the adventure there, for another to enjoy." [Correspondence from Lake Superior Scuba Divers, Duluth, Minnesota, to Superintendent, Isle Royale NP, June 18, 1973]. Since this maturing ethic coincided with National Park Service philosophy, it gradually emerged as the new community standard at Isle Royale.

Park rangers began a more active role in monitoring artifact removal, while educating the diving and non-diving public about the importance of submerged cultural resources. A registration form was introduced for assessing diving activity and interpretative programs created to visually enhance divers' experiences on shipwreck remains. Although these

measures helped awaken the perception of non-divers and provided new information to divers, a real understanding of Isle Royale's underwater resources required a look below.

My first "intact" shipwreck dive took place on *Emperor*'s bow. Larry Sand, operator of the charter boat *Superior Diver,* picked me up at Amygdaloid Ranger Station. I was

*Isle Royale National Park's success in curbing artifact removal has been possible only through aid from the diving community. Information regarding theft from submerged cultural sites is seriously pursued by park rangers.*

preoccupied with a curious mixture of exhilaration and apprehension. It was an unusual day, sparkling with sunbeam reflections on placid blue lake waters. While I was suiting up, a look into those waters elicited a mirror image question on my face, "Why am I doing this?" The plunge broke that question with ever-widening ripples from the impact of a fully equipped diver wearing double cylinders. I sank quickly, overweighted and preoccupied with equalizing pressure in all those small, annoying sinus passages. I cleared the excess water from my mask. A sheer wall of riveted steel ship dominated silence that was broken only by uneasy gasps of air. At no other time does the routine act of breathing seem so vital and important. I was in the shadow of history, not as portrayed in books by someone else's perceptions, but in a living, dynamic environment.

*Emperor* seemed to speak, hesi-

tantly at first, of that dark June 1947 night when the vessel struck Canoe Rocks. "It wasn't my fault. Whoever steered such a course on that fair night laid me in this grave. For the 12 sailors taken with me, I can only offer my rusting bones as a memorial."

Any apprehension soon vanished as I floated less than gracefully around the bow wreckage and cargo holds filled with dark, reddish iron ore. I observed many artifacts in place, with a deep-felt satisfaction and hope that I would see them again. That dive ultimately led to an addiction, relieved only by continued diving.

From fellow sport divers I drew the excitement and inspiration necessary for a commitment to these underwater resources. Distrust evaporated as park staff "looked below" with the diving community and listened to suggestions as problem solvers, not as authorities. Cooperation was recognized as vital in coping with issues of safety and preservation.

In August 1976, Isle Royale witnessed the first recorded diver fatality, which occurred on *America.* Three years later, *Kamloops* and *Henry Chisholm* each claimed an unsuspecting victim. Rumors circulated that diving was to be prohibited in the park. Instead, the park chose a course still agreed to by sport divers.

"The two deaths this month have upset Isle Royale National Park Superintendent Jack Morehead, himself an avid diver. But he said the park service has no plans to restrict or eliminate scuba diving. 'While diving is considered safe,' Morehead said, 'there are certain hazards that divers — like mountain climbers — accept.' " [*Duluth News-Tribune,* 8/25/79]

Isle Royale National Park's success in curbing artifact removal has been possible only through aid from the diving community. Information regarding theft from submerged cultural sites is seriously pursued by park rangers. During 1980, the

*The* Glenlyon *wreck is documented during underwater research by the Submerged Cultural Resources Unit. The ship sank on October 31, 1924, northeast of Menagerie Island near Isle Royale.* Photo by Mitch Kezar, Submerged Cultural Resources Unit

National Park Service Submerged Cultural Resources Unit (SCRU) commenced a six-season research project to study Isle Royale's underwater environment. As professional archaeologists and avid divers, they documented shipwrecks with video tape, slides and illustrations. The SCRU policy of "non-destructive" archaeology, while counter to popular conceptions of the profession, provides for continued exploration by the public. Excavation will be attempted only when imminent destruction threatens a site and proper conservation and curatorship of artifacts are assured. A final report on the "Maritime Archaeology of Isle Royale National Park" will set a standard for management of underwater preserves throughout the United States.

Educational techniques such as park-diving brochures and an underwater self-guiding interpretive trail already show promise. A confusing disarray of wooden timbers and cargo was the obvious fate for *Monarch,* as Captain Robertson reeled under shock in a December encounter with Blake Point. Water-

proof guide in hand, a diver can now untangle *Monarch's* remains with greater understanding of that Great Lakes package freighter, of which there are no operating examples today. To ensure safe access and eliminate anchor damage on Isle Royale shipwrecks, park-maintained moorings were attached to all major shipwreck sites in 1986. Diving charter vessels are available to visitors under park permit; this assures some degree of control over services.

During the summer of 1985, sport divers were involved in operational diving through the Volunteer-In-Parks program. Underwater research methods including archaeological site survey, scientific illustration and video or photo documentation were shared through participation. In addition, the National Oceanic and Atmospheric Administration research vessel *Seward Johnson* briefly searched for the missing bow section of *Algoma,* lost over 100 years ago. *Algoma* provided a necessary transportation link westward to Thunder Bay, Ontario, before completion of Canada's transcontinental railway. Although

bow remains were not located, a videotape program on *Algoma,* sponsored by the Public Broadcasting System, Duluth, was produced by Thunder Bay volunteer Scott McWilliam.

The Submerged Cultural Resources Unit returned to Isle Royale in 1986 with staff of the National Geographic Society to document the steel freighter *Kamloops*. Lost for 50 years, *Kamloops* was located in August 1977 by Minneapolis sport divers in water exceeding 170 feet in depth. Remote operating vehicles were used by the National Geographic Society to obtain still and video photography. These miniature, remote-controlled submersibles eliminated deployment of divers on *Kamloops,* with the promise to make underwater survey more efficient and much safer on deep-water archaeological sites.

In 1984, Isle Royale shipwrecks were listed on the National Register of Historic Places, confirming the significance of these sites. Isle Royale is a pioneering experience and an example of how underwater preservation can work. □

# SHIPWRECKS
## of LAKE SUPERIOR

| NAME | DATE | CLASS | LENGTH | CAUSE | NAME | DATE | CLASS | LENGTH | CAUSE |
|---|---|---|---|---|---|---|---|---|---|
| 1. Thomas Wilson | June 7, 1902 | Steel steamer | 308' | Collision | 12. Emperor | June 4, 1947 | Steel steamer | 525' | Strand |
| 2. Benjamin B. Noble | April 28, 1914 | Steel steamer | 239' | Foundered | 12. Chester A. Congdon | Nov. 6, 1918 | Steel steamer | 532' | Strand |
| 3. Niagra | June 4, 1904 | Wooden tug | 130' | Stranded | 13. Monarch | Dec. 6, 1906 | Wooden steamer | 240' | Strand |
| 4. Samual P. Ely | Oct. 29, 1896 | Wooden schooner | 200' | Stranded | 14. Maggie McRae | May 30, 1888 | Wooden schooner | 150' | Found |
| 5. Madeira | Nov. 28, 1905 | Steel schooner | 436' | Stranded | 15. Theano | Nov. 17, 1906 | Steel steamer | 255' | Strand |
| 6. Hesper | May 3, 1905 | Wooden steamer | 250' | Stranded | 16. Neebing | Sept. 24, 1937 | Steel steamer | 193' | Explos |
| 7. George M. Cox | May 27, 1933 | Steel steamer | 259' | Stranded | 17. Gunilda | August 31, 1911 | Steel steamer | 200' | Strand |
| 7. Chisholm | Oct. 20, 1898 | Wooden steamer | 265' | Stranded | 18. Judge Hart | Nov. 28, 1942 | Steel steamer | 250' | Strand |
| 7. Cumberland | July 23, 1877 | Wooden steamer | 204' | Stranded | 19. Barge 115 (whaleback) | Dec. 18, 1899 | Steel barge | 256' | Strand |
| 8. America | June 7, 1928 | Steel steamer | 200' | Stranded | 20. Strathmore | Nov. 14, 1906 | Wooden steamer | 205' | Strand |
| 9. Kamloops | Dec. 7, 1927 | Steel steamer | 250' | Foundered | 21. Panther | June 27, 1916 | Wooden steamer | 248' | Collisi |
| 10. Glenlyon | Oct. 31, 1924 | Steel steamer | 328' | Stranded | 22. Samuel Mather | Nov. 22, 1891 | Wooden steamer | 246' | Collisi |
| 11. Algoma | Nov. 7, 1885 | Steel steamer | 270' | Stranded | 23. Sagamore | July 29, 1901 | Steel barge | 308' | Collisi |

94

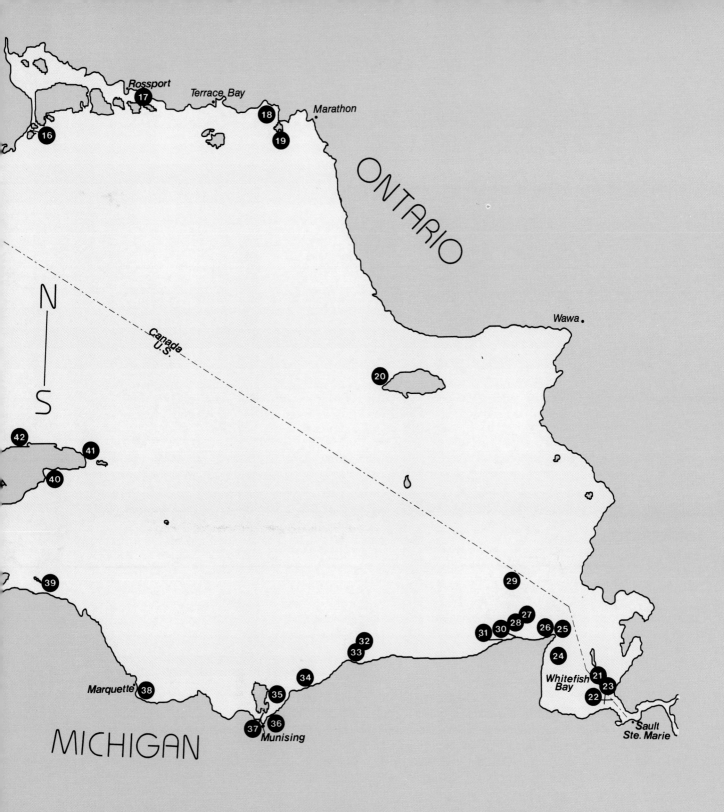

ONTARIO

Rossport
Terrace Bay
Marathon

Wawa

N
S

Canada
U.S.

MICHIGAN

Marquette

Whitefish
Bay

Sault
Ste. Marie

Munising

| | DATE | CLASS | LENGTH | CAUSE | NAME | DATE | CLASS | LENGTH | CAUSE |
|---|---|---|---|---|---|---|---|---|---|
| h | Aug. 28, 1926 | Wooden steamer | 202' | Foundered | 37. Granada | about 1870 | Wooden schooner | 150' | Unknown |
| na | Sept. 17, 1892 | Wooden steamer | 191' | Collision | 38. Charles Kershaw | Sept. 28, 1895 | Wooden steamer | 223' | Stranded |
| n B. Cowle | July 12, 1909 | Steel steamer | 420' | Collision | 39. George Nester | April 30, 1909 | Wooden schooner | 180' | Stranded |
| on | Nov. 22, 1919 | Wooden steamer | 186' | Stranded | 40. Langham | Oct. 23, 1910 | Wooden steamer | 281' | Fire |
| n Mitchell | July 10, 1911 | Steel steamer | 420' | Collision | 41. Altadoc | Dec. 7, 1927 | Steel steamer | 365' | Stranded |
| M. Osborne | July 27, 1884 | Wooden steamer | 178' | Collision | 42. William C. Moreland | Oct. 18, 1910 | Steel steamer | 580' | Stranded |
| und Fitzgerald | Nov. 10, 1975 | Steel steamer | 729' | Foundered | 43. Maplehurst | Nov. 30, 1922 | Steel steamer | 230' | Stranded |
| M. Drake | Oct. 2, 1901 | Wooden steamer | 201' | Collision | 44. Panama | Nov. 21, 1906 | Wooden steamer | 275' | Stranded |
| na | Sept. 1, 1859 | Wooden steamer | 200' | Foundered | 45. Lucerne | Nov. 18, 1886 | Wooden schooner | 195' | Foundered |
| . Parker | Sept. 1, 1903 | Wooden steamer | 246' | Foundered | 46. Fin McCool | 1964 | Barge | 135' | Abandoned |
| wa | Nov. 30, 1929 | Steel steamer | 251' | Stranded | 47. Fedora | Sept. 20, 1901 | Wooden steamer | 282' | Fire |
| erior | Oct. 29, 1856 | Wooden steamer | 184' | Stranded | 48. Pretoria | Sept. 2, 1905 | Wooden schooner | 338' | Foundered |
| man Hettler | Nov. 23, 1926 | Wooden steamer | 210' | Stranded | 49. Sevona | Sept. 2, 1905 | Steel streamer | 372' | Stranded |
| h Moore | July 13, 1889 | Wooden steamer | 223' | Collision | 50. Mayflower | June 2, 1891 | Wooden Schooner | 147' | Foundered |

# About the Authors

**Thom Holden** frequently describes himself as "a certified, card-carrying non-diver with an intense interest in Lake Superior shipwrecks, especially those around Isle Royale." Currently the assistant to the curator at Duluth's Canal Park Visitor Center and Marine Museum, Thom has worked with the National Park Service at Isle Royale and Apostle Islands National Lakeshore on various shipwreck projects. Known for the extent and accuracy of his research, Thom has assisted the NPS Submerged Cultural Resources Unit, the Ontario Government and the National Geographic Society. In 1986, Thom published *Above and Below*, an illustrated history of lighthouses and shipwrecks of Isle Royale. He was contributing editor on Dr. Julius F. Wolff Jr.'s *Lake Superior Shipwrecks.* He lives with his wife and daughter in Superior, Wisconsin.

**C. Patrick "Pat" Labadie,** curator of the U.S. Army Corps of Engineers Canal Park Visitors Center and Marine Museum at Duluth, Minnesota, is widely known for his flair for dramatizing history. Coming to Duluth from the Dossin Marine Museum at Detroit, Michigan, he transformed the concept of a marine museum into a living display of Lake Superior history. Under his guidance, the Visitors Center has become the most visited point in Minnesota, depicting to the casual traveler the gripping reality of lake activities. Pat's work has been widely published. He lives in Duluth.

**James Marshall,** publisher of *Lake Superior Magazine,* combines shipwreck examination with his fascination for the early mining activity of Lake Superior. Aboard his boat, *Skipper Sam II,* he has traced and described many early events of the north shore. After learning to dive in the early 1960s, he purchased the sunken *America,* described in this publication. Marshall's extensive library includes dozens of taped interviews with early mining and shipping folk, as well as early residents from around the lake. He has already begun the extensive research necessary to publish a sequel to this volume. He resides in Duluth.

**Frederick Stonehouse** is a captain for the Corps of Engineers, Michigan National Guard, as well as author of several important contributions to Lake Superior shipwreck lore. These include *Munising Shipwrecks, Went Missing, Isle Royale Shipwrecks, 15 Vessels That Disappeared On Lake Superior* and *The Wreck of the Edmund Fitzgerald.* Fred has earned a master of arts degree in American History from Northern Michigan University at Marquette, Michigan. His work has been published in numerous magazines and newspapers, including *Skin Diver, Divers International Divers Guide, Lake Superior Magazine* and *Dive* magazine. He is a member of the Great Lakes Historical and Marquette County Historical societies, the Lake Superior Marine Museum Association, the Alger Underwater Preserve Committee and is a director of the Marquette Maritime Museum. He makes his home in Flushing, Michigan.

**Ken Vrana,** formerly a research diving technician with the National Park Service Submerged Cultural Resources Unit, is a graduate of Michigan State University, where he majored in parks management. He served as a park ranger at Isle Royale National Park from 1976 to 1984, during which time he became a skilled diver, visiting all of the shipwrecks and historic sites of the island. His professional goal is the preservation of the Great Lakes basin and our environment. He travels throughout the continental United States, Alaska and Pacific territories on archaeological and technical diving projects. He currently works for Michigan Sea Grant

**Paul von Goertz** is an advertising and public relations executive with his own Duluth firm. A diver for many years, he has written a number of accounts of his underwater activities. He has served as a member of the Duluth Marine Museum artifacts committee. In recent years, Paul has given up diving due to an underwater situation which forced him into a panic, as described in his article on the *Thomas Wilson*. He lives in Knife River, Minnesota, with his wife and family.

**Dr. Julius F. Wolff, Jr.** completed his doctorate at the University of Minnesota in 1949 in political science. Joining the faculty of the University of Minnesota, Duluth, he retired as a professor in 1986. He served four years in the U. S. Army during World War II, continuing in the U.S. Army Reserve, retiring as a Colonel in 1975.

His maternal ancestors arrived by ship in 1866. His mother worked for a mining firm and his father was a mining engineer for the predecessor of U.S. Steel, both firms being tied to shipping on the Great Lakes. An assignment from the graduate school of the University of Minnesota to pursue shipping and ship accident activities on a part-time basis led to years of exploration of the lake. He has discovered and documented over 350 wrecks.

As a volunteer Boy Scout leader in the 1950s and 1960s, Dr. Wolff recruited a number of young men for Lake Superior shipwreck hunts. His work has been published in *Telescope* and *Inland Seas.* Long active in the Great Lakes Historical Society, he is presently assistant editor of its publication, *Inland Seas.*

His book *The Shipwrecks of Lake Superior* was first published in 1979. A larger expanded volume was published in 1990, a joint effort of the Lake Superior Marine Museum Association and Lake Superior Port Cities Inc., publishers of *Lake Superior Magazine.* It is the result of 30 years of research and is considered the finest work of its kind. Dr. Wolff makes his home in Duluth.

# *Index to* Shipwrecks of Lake Superior

Bold-faced page number indicates entry throughout story.
Italics page number indicates author/photographer of story.

# For Additional Reading

## Dr. Julius F. Wolff Jr.'s Lake Superior Shipwrecks

The only comprehensive summary of the maritime history of Lake Superior – or any Great Lake – Dr. Julius F. Wolff's *Lake Superior Shipwrecks* is a reflection of more than 30 years of research. It chronicles more than 1,700 known disasters and accidents that have occurred since commercial shipping began. Accounts are current through the December 1989 grounding of the Coast Guard cutter *Mesquite*. Contributing Editor, Thom Holden. *Endorsed and registered by the Association for Great Lakes Maritime History.*

304 pages, more than 200 historical photographs, footnoted, index of more than 1,700 ships, glossary, maps and charts, complete bibliography. Beautifully bound, available in hardcover and softcover versions. 8½" x 11."

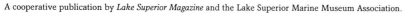

A cooperative publication by *Lake Superior Magazine* and the Lake Superior Marine Museum Association.

**Frank Barcus**
*Fresh Water Fury*
Wayne State University Press, 1960

**Dana Thomas Bowen**
*Lore of the Lakes*
Daytona Beach, Florida, 1940
Current publisher: Freshwater Press Inc.

*Memories of the Lakes*
Daytona Beach, Florida, 1946
Current publisher: Freshwater Press Inc.

*Shipwrecks of the Lakes*
Daytona Beach, Florida, 1952
Current publisher: Freshwater Press Inc.

**Dwight Boyer**
*Ghost Ships of the Great Lakes*
Dodd, Mead Company, 1968
Current publisher: Freshwater Press Inc.

*Great Stories of the Great Lakes*
Dodd, Mead Company, 1966
Current publisher: Freshwater Press Inc.

*True Tales of the Great Lakes*
Dodd, Mead Company, 1971
Current publisher: Freshwater Press Inc.

**Mary Frances Doner**
*The Salvager*
Ross and Haines Inc., 1955

**Elmer Engman**
*In the Belly of the Whale*
Innerspace, Duluth, Minnesota, 1976

*Shipwreck Guide to the Western Half of Lake Superior*
Innerspace, Duluth, Minnesota, 1976

**Mac Frimodig**
*Shipwrecks Off Keweenaw*
Michigan Department of Natural Resources. Fort Wilkins Natural History Association, 1974

**Harlan Hatcher**
*The Great Lakes*
Oxford University Press, 1944

**Walter Havighurst**
*The Great Lakes Reader*
Macmillan Company, 1966

**Havighurst** continued
*The Long Ships Passing*
Macmillan Company, 1943

**Thomas Holden**
*Above and Below*
Isle Royale Natural History Association, 1985

**James K. Jamison**
*By Cross and Anchor*
St. Anthony Guild Press, 1946

**James M. Keller**
*The "Unholy" Apostles*
Apostle Island Press, 1984

**Robert E. Lee**
*Edmund Fitzgerald, 1957–1975*
Great Lakes Maritime Institute, 1977

**Daniel J. Lenihan**
*\*Shipwrecks of Isle Royale National Park*
Lake Superior Port Cities Inc., 1994

**T. Morris Longstreth**
*The Lake Superior Country*
The Century Company, 1924

**Grace Lee Nute**
*Lake Superior*
Bobbs-Merrill Company, 1944

**William Ratigan**
*Great Lakes Shipwrecks and Survivals*
William B. Eerdsman Company, 1960
Current publisher: Freshwater Press Inc.

**Hamilton Ross**
*La Pointe*
North Central Publishing Company, 1960

**William E. Scott**
*The Wreck of the Lafayette*
Scott-Mitchell Publishing Company, 1959

**Frederick Stonehouse**
*Isle Royale Shipwrecks*
Avery Color Studios, 1974

*Keweenaw Shipwrecks*
Avery Color Studios, 1988

*Lake Superior's "Shipwreck Coast"*
Avery Color Studios, 1985

**Stonehouse** continued
*Marquette Shipwrecks*
Haboridge Press, 1974

*Munising Shipwrecks*
Avery Color Studios, 1983

*Went Missing II*
Avery Color Studios, 1984

*The Wreck of the Edmund Fitzgerald*
Avery Color Studios, 1977

*\*Shipwreck of the Mesquite*
Lake Superior Port Cities Inc., 1991

*\*Wreck·Ashore: The United States Life-Saving Service on the Great Lakes*
Lake Superior Port Cities Inc., 1994

**Homer Wells**
*History of Accidents, Casualties and Wrecks on Lake Superior*
Corps of Engineers, U.S. Army, 1938. Typewritten manuscript in Duluth Public Library

**Dr. Julius F. Wolff Jr.**
*The Ships and Duluth*
In *Duluth – Sketches of the Past.*
Duluth American Revolution Bicentennial Commission, 1976

*\*Lake Superior Shipwrecks*
Lake Superior Marine Museum Association. Lake Superior Port Cities Inc., 1990

## Periodicals

*Lake Superior Magazine\** is a bimonthly full-color publication about Lake Superior. This magazine is available through subscription from the publishers of this book. Also available is the *Lake Superior Travel Guide*. Many of the Great Lakes marine and historical societies publish newsletters and booklets. The *Nor'Easter*, published by the Lake Superior Marine Museum, Duluth; the Marquette (Michigan) *Maritime Museum Bulletin*; and *Lake Log Chips*, Bowling Green State University (Ohio) are but a few. *Inland Seas*, the quarterly bulletin of The Great Lakes Historical Society, Vermilion, Ohio, is generally regarded as the most complete single authoritative source of contemporary and historical information. Elmer Engman's *Inner Space Diving Letter* is an important newsletter for divers.

*\*Available through*
*Lake Superior Magazine*
*Product Catalog.*
*P.O. Box 16417*
*Duluth, Minnesota 55816-0417*
*800-635-0544*
*Call for current prices.*